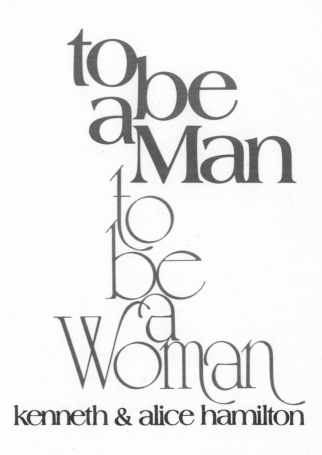

to be a Man to be a Woman

kenneth & alice hamilton

Abingdon • Nashville

TO BE A MAN—TO BE A WOMAN

ISBN 0-687-42149-7

Scripture quotations unless otherwise noted are from the Revised
Standard Version of the Bible, copyrighted 1964 and 1952 by the
Division of Christian Education, National Council of Churches, and
are used by permission.

Scripture quotations noted NEB are from The New English Bible ©
the Delegates of the Oxford University Press and the Syndics of
the Cambridge University Press 1961, 1970. Reprinted by permission.

Scripture quotations noted KJV are from the King James Version.

MANUFACTURED BY THE PARTHENON PRESS AT
NASHVILLE, TENNESSEE, UNITED STATES OF AMERICA

acknowledgments

1. From *The Christian Response to the Sexual Revolution* by David R. Mace (Abingdon Press, 1970), pp. 81-82. Copyright © 1970 by Abingdon Press.

2. From *The Zeal of Thy House* by Dorothy Sayers, in *Religious Drama I: Five Plays*, ed. by Marvin Halverson (Meridian Books, Inc., 1957), pp. 298-299. Copyright © 1937 Dorothy L. Sayers. Used by permission.

3. From *The Jerusalem Bible*, copyright © 1966 by Darton, Longman & Todd, Ltd. and Doubleday & Company, Inc. Used by permission of the publisher.

4. From *Oliver Twist* by Charles Dickens (Dodd, Mead & Company, 1941), p. 520.

5. From "The Subjection of Women" by John Stuart Mill, in *Women's Liberation and Literature*, ed. Elaine Showalter (Harcourt Brace Jovanovich, Inc., 1971), p. 34. Copyright © 1971 Harcourt Brace Jovanovich, Inc.

6. From "A Perfect Day for Bananafish" by J. D. Salinger in *Nine Stories* (Random House, Inc., The Modern Library, 1953), p. 15. Copyright, 1953 by J. D. Salinger.

7. From *The Death of a Salesman* by Arthur Miller (The Viking Press, Inc., 1949), p. 56. Copyright 1949 by Arthur Miller. Reprinted by permission of The Viking Press, Inc.

8. From *Creation and Fall* by Dietrich Bonhoeffer, trans. by John C. Fletcher (SCM Press, Ltd. 1966), p. 84. Copyright © 1966 by SCM Press, Ltd.

9. Reprinted from *The Hymnal* (1940), No. 324. Copyright 1940, 1943 by The Church Pension Fund. Used by permission.

10. From *An Offering of Uncles: The Priesthood of Adam and the Shape of the World* by Robert Farrar Capon (Sheed and Ward, Inc., 1967), p. 131. Copyright © Sheed and Ward, Inc., 1967.

11. From *Couples* by John Updike (Alfred A. Knopf, 1968), p. 451. Copyright © 1968 by John Updike.

12. *Couples*, p. 106.

13. *Couples*, p. 151.

Corresponding superior numbers in the text indicate the location of each excerpt.

contents

to be a Man

to be a Woman

1
men & women in a time of sexual revolution

Scripture: Ephesians 4:1-16
> Paul speaks of our vocation in the church. Individuals play different parts but grow toward maturity through working together, united by love and a common purpose.

Kenneth: Since we are going to speak with one voice through the rest of this book, we should make clear from the start that we are really two people.

Alice: And I don't always see eye to eye with you. I've lived with you for twenty-eight years; I've loved you for more. But we argue.

Kenneth: Yes. For instance, I don't think you are willing to give men the benefit of the doubt where their attitude toward women is concerned. Your feminist attitude won't allow you to think that men are ever *not* biased against women.

Alice: I would not trust even you to give the women's point of view. Men always assume that they are more rational and impartial than women. They don't listen to women because they don't believe women have anything important to say. It's rather easy to be "impartial" if you're only stating a man's bias. Your reasoning has a lot of rationalization in it.

Kenneth: Anyway, Alice and I manage to keep finding things to disagree about, and that means life is never dull. But what we have written here about the problems of man-woman relationships and how we should set about solving them is what we both believe. We speak from a joint conviction, not from a watered-down compromise.

Alice: And it's not theory—for me, at any rate. I've spent years of my life looking after a home and family, and years as a professional woman. I know a little about both lives. Men have little tension between work and family. Women do have this tension—and precious little value in most people's eyes if they don't earn money.

Kenneth: My own career has been divided into two periods also: first as a minister in the pastorate and later as a teacher of theology. But that division of career is perhaps less important in a personal way than the division of being the husband of a woman-at-home and then the husband of a woman-at-work. The practical adjustments of the change-over were not very demanding. Our children were well on the way to being independent when Alice started her academic career again. But the mental adjustments were considerable.

Alice: I went back to work for money. We needed it, and I had a chance to help out. I did not expect to stay at work, but the family helped me to do so. They knew I needed to grow up, and it took more than a home to start me growing.

So now we're trying to tell you what we believe about men and women. We would not have written any differently if this book were meant for our family or for our students. We write from a biblical perspective, not as a matter of dragging in religion, but because, for both of us, this is the only way we know. We are telling you about the human situation as we see it, and we believe that our lives can be explained only from beyond ourselves. Any other viewpoint leaves too much to be explained.

THE SEXUAL REVOLUTION

By definition, men and women are adult members of the human species capable of sexual union. So the place of sexuality in our North American society is the first topic to be discussed as we think about the man-woman relation today.

Everywhere around us is talk of the Sexual Revolution. *Time* magazine devoted a cover story to it as early as 1969, and almost any paper or magazine we pick up is likely to carry at least one article discussing some aspect of this revolution. In spite of all the publicity, there is still a great deal of vagueness about what the Sexual Revolution actually means.

Some people—perhaps the majority—think the Sexual Revolution means promiscuity, or what used to be called "free love." Certainly, there is reason for such a conclusion. Casual or short-term sex seems to be accepted as normal in the mass media these days. Where the barriers are not completely down, they are weakening visibly. An actress, whose role in a television soap opera portrays her as twice widowed and about to marry her third husband, was reported to have said, "I wish I could just take a lover without all the fuss of another marriage, but television isn't ready for that yet." Meanwhile, any number of women's magazines tell their readers how they can enjoy sex in styles usually thought of as belonging to the more scandalous circles in Hollywood.

Still, the ideal of faithfulness in marriage remains widely accepted, even by those who are ready to advocate unrestricted premarital sex. Some self-styled experts prophesy that the family as we know it will be gone before the end of this century. Yet, neither these prophesies nor the widely publicized experiments in communal living have affected to any marked extent the thinking of most North American adults. And promiscuity among the young, though apparently increasing, is by no means as widespread as the literature on the drugstore racks tries to make us believe.

The impact of the Sexual Revolution is not in its challenge to monogamous marriage. Rather, the Sexual Revolution has been most successful in its ability to sell the idea that there should be no limit to the extent to which sex can be made public and exploited for profit. The Sexual Revolution *may* have altered our sexual habits as a society, though to what extent we do not know. It definitely *has* altered our attitude toward sex.

One side of the Sexual Revolution has been healthy. It has done away with guilty silence about sex or evasion of discussion of the physical aspects of sex. Sexuality is a vital part of our existence, and the subject should be open for investigation and discussion just as is any other important topic. Another side of the revolution that is less healthy socially and perhaps destructive of human values is the concentration upon the sex act as though it were the only important aspect of sexuality. As a result, sex has been separated from the rest of life and turned into a commodity. Instead of recognizing sexuality as part of our total nature as human beings, and the sex act as one particularly intense expression of our sexual existence, we are encouraged to think of sex as a "thing." This "thing" we get pleasure from, directly (through sexual intercourse) or indirectly (through written or visual presentations of the sex act about which we fantasize). With this understanding of sex, we then begin to think that we are being cheated if we do not "get our money's worth" out of this "thing," as though it were a television set or an automobile. And here the commercial dealers in sex assure us they can help us, by supplying everything from manuals on sexual technique to movies showing scenes involving sex.

The excesses of the Sexual Revolution are not what matter most, though these get the publicity. In all likelihood, the recent surge of nudity and "realistic" sex on the stage and in movies is receding. Overexposure of anything, including frontal nudity, finally causes boredom. But the threat of permanent damage lies in separating the sex act from personhood and making it an end in itself. When sexual intercourse is thought to be primarily a pleasurable activity justified by technique and performance, as though it were water-skiing, it loses true human meaning. Sex becomes separated from the intimate personal qualities of affection, trust, and sacrificial love. When this happens, anti-social forms of sexuality, such as homosexuality, are regarded equally as valuable as socially profitable ones. Also, second-hand sex may become preferred to first-hand sex, because it demands much less individual effort. The choice of voyeurism (getting sexual satisfaction from seeing the sex organs or sex acts of others) instead of the actual experience could be the final end of a sick society.

WOMEN IN THE SEXUAL REVOLUTION

The Sexual Revolution seems to have come about quite recently and quite suddenly. Actually it is a breaking through to the surface of a vast social change that has been going on for well over a hundred years.

The famous Kinsey Report on the sexual behavior of American men and women created a great stir in the fifties. His Report showed that many people were pretending to accept traditional standards of sexual ethics, but, in fact, were behaving quite differently. This situation may have existed for ages before the Report was published. The same situation may have existed also in countries other than America. But seeing firm statistics shocked people considerably. And they were upset, too, by Dr. Kinsey's personal attitude toward his findings. He seemed to be saying that, if his figures showed how men and women were actually behaving, society should accept such facts as a *standard* of sexual morality.

The long-term Sexual Revolution, as we may call it, was connected with the movement for the emancipation of women. The public sign of the movement's success was the winning of the vote and entry of women into the professions. But the movement had a much more extensive program than that, and it was aimed primarily at changing the basic attitude of male superiority that had kept women subordinate to their fathers, brothers, and husbands. Women demanded to be recognized as full persons, not just in City Hall, but in the marriage bed as well.

Dr. David Mace, a veteran worker in marriage counseling, describes three distinct periods in the history of his work. In the first period, wives came to ask the counselor to persuade their husbands to moderate their excessive sexual demands. In the second period, the husbands came for advice. They were worried because their wives were so often sexually unresponsive. In the third period, the wives came again, this time to complain about their husbands' clumsiness in sexual technique.

Dr. Mace sees these three periods as three stages in the Sexual Revolution, with women advancing from passive recipients of male desires to persons expecting to receive as much fulfillment as men. Dr. Mace observes also that the spread of knowledge about contraceptives was actually more important in furthering women's rights than was the gaining of the vote. Women have to establish freedom in the home before they can make any use of the larger freedom in society. They cannot use their minds if their bodies give them no leisure.[1]

Dr. Mace is right. The real turning point in the Sexual Revolution came with birth control. Women were at last set free from the male will. No longer could the male force upon the female the alternative, "Breed, or abstain from sex." Now if men wished for children they had to obtain the willing cooperation of their wives. Women demanded to be considered equal partners in sexual intercourse. Sex was no longer recreation for the man and procreation for the woman. Both sexes could find self-fulfillment in sex.

WHAT IS SEX FOR?

Sexual freedom was by no means assured in the first half of the twentieth century. A fairly typical experience was contained in the remark of one husband that he and his wife had acquired six children through six different methods of birth control. With the arrival of oral contraception in the sixties, however, the goal of sexual freedom was at last in sight. Perhaps the Pill helped to convince people that the Sexual Revolution was real, for it was in the late sixties that the term *Sexual Revolution* became widely used.

The great impact of the Pill became apparent when Roman Catholics around the world criticized Pope Paul VI's pronouncement against birth control. Previously, statistics in America and Western Europe had shown that Roman Catholics were not very different from their Protestant neighbors in their actual use of birth control measures. But never before had Roman Catholics publicly opposed their church's official teaching.

Pope Paul VI also received much criticism in the press over the issue. He was said to have missed the chance of showing that Catholicism cared deeply about twentieth-century problems, particularly the problem of world over-population. People were disappointed too over his failure to state a clear and positive view of human sexuality. The Pope's pronouncement reinforced the image of the church as a male-dominated institution in which unmarried clergy dictated to the laity the sexual ethics they must accept without question. At the same time, a number of priests and nuns married, defying the authority of the church yet asserting that they had not left the church.

The fundamental question in the controversy was What is sex for, and how should Christians of the twentieth century, both Catholic and Protestant, understand their sexuality? Quite obviously, the twentieth century has not learned how to deal with sex or to use responsibly the sexual freedom it has won.

Churchmen are not the only ones who find contemporary sexual attitudes chaotic. Vance Packard, a sociologist who wrote a book entitled *The Sexual Wilderness,* is sure that the confusion in society over the roles of men and women is the most urgent unsettled question facing us today. The answer we give to this question will determine the future of the whole human race.

In all the frantic assertions that sexual freedom is the road to human happiness, there are few indications that our age has found either happiness or individual self-fulfillment. Instead, bitterness, cynicism, and increasing antagonism between the sexes is evident everywhere. Above all, persons despair that sexual freedom and social stability ever will be reconciled.

PROCREATION AND RECREATION

In the past, human sexuality was assumed to be for procreation and needed to be strictly regulated for the good of society. Today it is thought to be for recreation (that is, pleasure without intent to create) and to be left unregulated as far as possible for the good of the individual.

Sex approached as recreation is often referred to as "spiritual communion," or "creative self-fulfillment," or "finding personal identity." The terms simply indicate what the individual wants for himself—or what he likes to imagine he wants.

The two views of sexuality, procreation and recreation, have coincided more or less with the arranged marriage and the marriage by personal choice. The latter is usually supposed to be the result of "falling in love." But it may be simply a matter of finding someone with matching temperament and deciding marriage will work.

All previous ages were aware of the phenomenon of "falling in love." But, on the whole, falling in love was considered irrelevant or socially disastrous. Sex for recreation was permitted a man, provided it did not interfere with his social duties. Samson, for instance, could visit a prostitute (Judges 16:1) without anyone's being particularly concerned. But when he became emotionally involved with Delilah, who was in the pay of Israel's enemy, the Philistines, then everyone knew that only evil could come of his infatuation. A "grand passion" was admitted to be something rather splendid—Anthony's love for Cleopatra and Nelson's love for Lady Hamilton are two famous examples—but everyone agreed that such emotional extravagance must end tragically. A man should know better than to let his private feeling interfere with his public duties.

Today the Western World has a higher estimate of personality, both male and female, and estimates of sexual relationships solely on the basis of their social good are no longer possible. Arranged marriages seem to us to be especially intolerable. We would not wish to return to the old days in this regard. Yet the advance in individual freedom carries with it a danger that the social side of sexuality may be pushed into the background. Putting individual happiness first and well-being of society second offers a real threat to the very existence of the human community.

Often it is argued that an individual's sexual conduct is his (or her) own business, so long as no one else is being hurt. Yet sexuality is never just a matter between two individuals, because in every sexual act procreation is made either possible or impossible. The next generation is involved. Society cannot, for this reason, be indifferent to the sexual habits of its members. Militant feminists, for example, argue that a woman should have sole responsibility over her own body. If she becomes pregnant, she should have freedom to have an abortion. If she wishes to bear a child, she should have freedom to bring it up without reference to the father. The social implications of such demands are these: (1) that women, and women alone, are to hold the power of life and death over the next generation; and (2) that fathers are to have no responsibility for their children beyond the act of begetting them. Similarly, social recognition of homosexual unions would mean the sanctioning of physical relationships that can only be sterile; and it would encourage one-sex groupings within a two-sex community. These situations would be damaging to the social fabric.

MEN AND WOMEN IN SOCIETY

The social side of sexuality is just as important for men and women as individuals as it is for society as a whole. Persons are directly responsible for the quality of their own lives. They have much less control over the quality of life in their society. However, since the exercise of responsibility is always within a social setting, men and women discover that sexual responsibility cannot be separated from social responsibility.

Here individual good will, without a social perspective, is not enough. Individual feelings exist temporarily. A choice made one hour may be regretted the next. The one who is loved today may become an object of hatred tomorrow. But social duties exist permanently. Parents may cease loving each other, may feel that their marriage is dead, and may decide to bury it. But the children of a dead marriage do not disappear. They remain as living witness to their parents' choice of individual feelings over social affection or concern. A couple choosing legal divorce acknowledge their social obligations in the face of the law. But in a human sense, they have repudiated them, for they are denying their children their place within the society of the family. In effect, they are saying to their children: "Adults alone are persons, because they have freedom to let their feelings rule their choices. One day you, too, will be able to throw aside all obligations that you find inconvenient."

Of course, social duty and the quality of an individual's life belong together and support each other. Neither can exist by itself. Parents who have ceased to live in mutual trust and confidence, but who decide to stay together "for the sake of the children," may in fact inflict more pain upon their children than if they separated. Forcing a child to see, every moment of each day, that the family is a community in name only and that neither parent hopes for reconciliation is to weld social duty into a chain of frustration rather than a bond of peace. In such a situation, social affection should begin at a more fundamental level; it should start with the parents and their understanding of marriage, demanding a relationship based on a training in discipline and issuing in the glad self-sacrifice of love.

Talking about marriage being made by "love" and not by "laws" does not alter the fact that the love that depends on individual feelings and that is unable to accept permanent duties and responsibilities is love in name only. Love includes both individual and social affection. It can turn abstract "duty" into outgoing self-forgetfulness. To concentrate only upon one affection—individual or social—is to lose both. To deny one affection is to wipe out the other.

Our problems in knowing our roles as men and women lie partly outside ourselves, in the changes going on in society, particularly those changes brought about by the Sexual Revolution. But they also lie within ourselves, in our lack of understanding what our sexuality involves and how we should direct it toward cementing rather than dissolving the human community.

TEACHING-LEARNING SUGGESTIONS

Using These Suggestions
The following suggestions may be adapted in any way you wish
as you plan a lesson. The directions in dark type will give you
an idea of how each section might be used. You are not
expected to deal with all the ideas in the chapter, nor are you
expected to use all the suggestions or discuss all the questions.
Select the ideas, suggestions, and questions of most value to
your group.

Topic Question
Why is it essential to understand the God-given nature of our
sexuality as men or women?

Goal
Decide if and why it is important for you to answer the topic
question. You may want to reword the question or to write
your own. Then, decide what you want to find out in order to
answer your question.

Preview of the Lesson
(This outline of the main ideas in the chapter and the related
questions are to aid the leader who chooses the lecture-discussion method of teaching.)
  1. We live in a time of "sexual revolution."
     a. On one hand, the Sexual Revolution is marked by the
        open and public display of sexuality—the selling of sex.
     b. On the other hand, the Sexual Revolution has made
        sexuality a matter for investigation and discussion.
     c. Much present interest in sexuality focuses on the sex
        act, making it an end in itself and isolating sex from
        the rest of life.
  2. The Sexual Revolution has been closely connected with
     the emancipation of women; women seek to be recognized
     as full persons in every dimension of life.
     a. The advent of birth control marked a turning point in
        the Sexual Revolution and in women's emancipation. It
        freed women to experience sex as an avenue for self-
        expression and self-fulfillment.
     b. The Sexual Revolution and women's emancipation have
        clouded the understanding of the roles of men and
        women in society.
  3. Confusion about sexual attitudes and sexual roles threatens
     the stability of society.
  4. Sexuality is seen as procreation or recreation.
     a. Seen as procreation only, sexuality destroys the per-
        sonalities of men and women.
     b. Seen as recreation only, sexuality denies the natural
        fulfillment of sexuality and destroys personality.

c. Sexuality is never a private matter between two individuals; future generations are always involved.
5. Ultimately, persons are directly responsible for their own quality of life; each person must come to understand and live with his maleness or femaleness as a God-given dimension of the totality of life.

Related Questions to Discuss

1. Is it possible for a man to understand a woman's perspective, and a woman a man's perspective on life? Explain your answer.
2. What does the sexual revolution mean to you? How have your attitudes and ideas on sexuality changed over the years? What has caused these changes?
3. In what ways have you observed sexuality being turned into a commodity in entertainment, advertising, or contemporary literature?
4. Should *prevailing* sexual behavior set the moral standard for sexual behavior? Give reasons for your answer. What should set the moral standards for sexual behavior?
5. What does it mean to you to *recognize women as full persons?* How is this different from recognizing men as full persons?
6. Can a person experience wholeness without sexual self-expression and sexual fulfillment? Explain.
7. Might an individual completely understand his or her role as a man or a woman even though these roles are uncertain in society? Illustrate your answer.
8. What is the relationship between sexuality and "falling in love"?
9. In what specific ways is the next generation directly involved in every sexual act? Which partner in a sexual act should be responsible to and for the next generation?
10. In the area of his or her sexuality, what social responsibilities does an individual have? How do these responsibilities differ from what the writers call "individual good will"? (See page 19.)

(The suggestions below are designed to aid leaders and groups desiring a variety of teaching-learning techniques. Choose and adapt those suggestions best suited to the needs of your group.)

Begin

Begin this session—and this study—by posting this question on chalkboard or newsprint: "What does it mean to be a man or to be a woman?" Explain to the group members that this question will be the focus of the entire study and that answers should seek to explain maleness and femaleness apart from society's stereotypes. Keep this question posted.

As a whole group, brainstorm a list of clichés or often-heard phrases that seem to stereotype men and women. You'll think of "A woman has to have the last word," "Behind every great man is a great woman," "Isn't that just like a man?" and many more. What kind of overall image of men and women comes through these phrases? Are these phrases accurate descriptions of men and women? If your answer is *no*, then why do persons continue to use these phrases?

Continue

In pairs, discuss the differences between using sex in advertising and the legitimate open investigation and discussion of sexuality. After your discussion, as a whole group try to agree on a set of guidelines for judging whether a certain book, film, or discussion isolates sex from the rest of life or helps persons understand more completely the God-createdness of sexuality.

The writers of this book say, "Society cannot be indifferent to the sexual habits of its members." Let each person answer in turn: What does this mean to you in terms of censorship, the availability of contraceptives, planned parenthood, and so on?

Conclude

Close this session by offering sentence prayers of thanksgiving for something you appreciate about being a man or being a woman.

2
the human self & the kingdom of God

RICK SMOLAN

Scripture: Mark 1:14-22

> **The ministry of Jesus began with the preaching of the Kingdom and the calling of disciples. How does our vocation as men and women relate to Jesus' call to us to be his disciples?**

What is a wife to do if her husband refuses to consider her a person who is adult and responsible but treats her instead as one of his possessions—someone he likes to have around the house, *his* wife and the mother of *his* children?

Nora Helmer had that problem. Her husband was always proud that she was very "feminine," and even a little childish in her tastes. After he was promoted to bank manager, he was happy to think that they could afford to live without pinching pennies and that Nora could enjoy a few luxuries. But one day he learned that, at a time when he was very ill and money was needed desperately, Nora had borrowed some money in circumstances that could lead to scandal. She was paying it off little by little. Without considering the reason that had driven Nora to take the risk, and thinking that his good name and position were in danger, her husband attacked her viciously. Then when it appeared that there was to be no scandal after all, he assumed that everything he had said could now be forgotten. Nora did not think so. She was seeing her husband for the first time. She had been willing to risk her reputation and peace of mind for his welfare, so that they could share good and bad times together. But she learned that he had never cared for her in her own right, had never thought of her as a partner. He had cast her in the role of a respectable manager of his home, someone he could show off as a devoted wife and mother, who was also an attractive "doll." Nora could not continue to live in a marriage based on such inequality. She was no longer content to live up to her husband's image of what a wife should be. She told him that she was leaving him and would not come back. Then, to his amazement, she walked out of the house, slamming the door behind her.

GOING OUT AND COMING IN

Nora Helmer is a character in Henrik Ibsen's play *A Doll's House*. If the shot fired at Concord in 1775 rang around the world, Nora's slamming of her "doll's house" door rang around the world in 1879, the year Ibsen's play was on the stage. It was the first public declaration of women's liberation. No one before had suggested so directly that a woman might be justified in putting her dignity as a human being before her duties as wife and mother. Ibsen's contemporaries were almost as shocked by Nora's action as Nora's husband, Torvald Helmer, had been in the play.

In the story of Nora's discovery of her need to be recognized as a person in her own right, the playwright Ibsen shone a searchlight into a dark corner of life in his day. He showed how a pretense at moral virtue often served as a cloak for immorality and how slogans about the sanctity of family life could be used to excuse male egotism and its exploitation of female "dependence." The sheltered existence that women led in the home might seem to be a privileged life, one that encouraged their femininity. In truth, it was as likely to be a limiting and a limited life, preventing them from taking an active part in society and giving them no protection against males who happened to be tyrants in their own families.

Although Ibsen pointed to the existence of a social problem, he did little more than that. Certainly, he did not solve the problem. But he did suggest that women might refuse to accept the "doll's house" role and walk away to find their own freedom. They could "go out" of an intolerable situation. But "going out" of one place serves little purpose unless one can afterwards "come in" to another, better place.

We still have not found any real solution to the problem raised by Ibsen nearly a hundred years ago. True, the labor market today is more open to women to make careers for themselves than it was in his day. Opportunities for women to earn a living then were limited to certain types of work, most with low pay. Today, most skilled work and practically all the professions are open to women, although strong prejudice still exists in some quarters. "Going out" is easier now, but "coming in" remains a problem. Uniting a career with a family and a home is still a problem with no clear resolution. Most women have to choose between the two.

Men still speak of women as "dolls." And women, even career women, usually try to look as though they were dainty flowers, far removed from anything suggesting work or efficiency. The female models used by advertisers to sell products of all kinds never give the impression that they would want to walk out of a husband's or boy friend's house and slam the door behind them. Have we really come to terms with a view of women that thinks of the feminine other than as a doll-like object?

JESUS AND THE KINGDOM OF GOD

When women want to walk out of a society dominated by men, it is not just a woman's problem. Something is wrong with the world of men too. Such a situation suggests that human beings, men and women alike, have forgotten that human life depends upon both male and female coming together and living together. If the man does not recognize the woman as a being who is fully human and a partner in the human enterprise, then he diminishes his own humanity. If the woman's only hope is in refusing to share the male world, then she cuts herself off from her own humanity in the process.

No solution can be found by looking only at the male side or only at the female side of the problem. This is a problem for the human self—the male and the female equally. We have to strive for a society where both sexes can "come in" and find themselves at home.

Such a society has never existed fully. We can look through history and fail to find any community where male and female humanity have lived in perfect harmony. Anthropologists can tell us of patriarchal and of matriarchal societies that have worked quite well, up to a point and under certain conditions. But no social organization can guarantee harmony and no formula will give us a lasting peace from the "war" of the sexes.

When Jesus began his ministry he came preaching the kingdom of God. The Kingdom was for humanity; men and women alike were called. Divisions no longer existed. When the apostle Paul spoke of the divisions that were overcome through Jesus Christ, he explicitly mentioned the division between male and female (Galatians 3:28).

Jesus laid down no schemes for social reorganization or blueprints for a new social order when he came preaching the Kingdom. (For this reason, perhaps the rule of God is a better translation than the kingdom of God.) His words were, "Repent and believe in the gospel." He demanded, first of all, a change of heart and an admission that we have not been living according to the will of God for humanity. The change is to come from within, but it is not to stay there. This change is to be more than spiritual; it is to touch everyday life. Jesus made it perfectly clear that those to whom the gospel had come were to recognize certain human obligations as absolutely binding. They were to love their neighbor, not merely in a spiritual sense, but in practical ways. Finding a way to heal a quarrel with a brother was more important than making a religious offering (Matthew 5:24). Service to "the least" in society was equivalent to service to the Master himself (Matthew 25: 40). When Jesus contrasted the behavior of self-centered people with what he expected of his disciples, he declared: "It shall not be so among you. . . ." That declaration is still true.

When Jesus announced the kingdom of God, he announced a way of "coming in" to a new human relationship with others.

HUMANITY CREATED MALE AND FEMALE

The Kingdom that Jesus proclaimed was "not of this world." That is, it would not come about through human rules or regulations but would be the result of God's touching human hearts and reshaping human lives.

One of the social practices that Jesus spoke against was divorce. According to Mark 10:11-12 Jesus prohibited divorce absolutely. According to Matthew 5:31-32 and 19:9 he allowed one exception—where sexual infidelity was the cause.

Since divorce in those days was most often put into effect by the husband, the wife's social position and personal security were most threatened by the practice. Yet Jesus did not argue on the basis of hardships or of the rights of the wronged party. He based what he said on the nature of humanity as God had created mankind. "He who made them from the beginning made them male and female" (Matthew 19:4); husband and wife were one flesh. Their unity was the act of their Creator, and no mere man-made expedient.

Thus Jesus linked human marriage to the original will of God for the unity of the human family. The union of husband and wife in marriage was a visible symbol of the unity of maleness and femaleness present in humanity. The dissolution of such a union reversed the intention of creation.

Jesus called unjustified divorce sought for the sake of remarriage *adultery,* making it an offense against the seventh commandment. In this way he emphasized that divorce is contrary to God's will. Man was not to part those whom God had joined. In the Old Testament the word *adultery* is often used to describe Israel's faithlessness to God, as in turning to worship the gods of her heathen neighbors. Jesus spoke in much the same way when he referred to the people of his day as "an evil and adulterous generation" (Matthew 12:39). When used in connection with divorce, the word *adultery* was more directly linked to sexual unfaithfulness, of course; but those who heard Jesus speak must have understood that the wider meaning was included also. This breach of the seventh commandment was more than a breach of faith between two persons—it was a clear denial of the rule of God, a sin disrupting God's kingdom.

In teaching about the kingdom of God, Jesus talked about the way in which God had "in the beginning" created humanity in the double form of male and female. God intended mankind to live in unity; therefore, the union of man and woman in marriage was to be the foundation of all human unity, to uphold the rule of God over mankind and to fulfill the design of creation.

Under the rule of God all men would be faithful to their Creator, loving him and their neighbors. On the human level such faithfulness would be reflected in the faithfulness of husband and wife. Adultery on the one level was closely connected with adultery on the other level.

RECOGNIZING GOD'S WILL FOR HUMANITY

The Kingdom is made possible through repentance. Human laws and institutions cannot bring about the unity of persons and the freedom from adultery that are the basis of marriage. These good gifts are the result of remembering our humanity as God created it to be, and of seeking for-

30

giveness for our lack of faithfulness to our Creator and to our fellows.

Thus commanding faithfulness by law does not get us very far. Jesus told his hearers that Moses allowed divorce "because of the hardness of your hearts" (Matthew 19:8, KJV). Where there are hard hearts, faithlessness will follow. For centuries, in countries predominantly Catholic, adultery was regarded lightly as long as the legal status of marriage was preserved "in the sight of men." Marriage looked after family succession and property, while private sexual morals were an individual matter in which no one expected perfection, at least among laymen. Protestants tried to establish a high standard for personal sexual ethics, while taking a less-than-absolute stand on divorce. For example, the Protestant attitude toward family morals during the age which we call "Victorian" was largely the result of the Evangelical movement of the early eighteenth century that preceded the Methodist revival. The effect of this attitude was to drive adultery underground rather than to banish it. The Victorian era was notable both for rigid public morals and for an enormous growth in prostitution.

Today we pride ourselves on being free from Victorian hypocrisy, and we smile at the out-of-date view that marriage is a matter of family pride and property. But simply adopting the morals of the hypocrite while giving up trying to hide one's action is not very much of an improvement. "At least he's honest about himself," we say of someone who does not make excuses for acting selfishly. But honesty is to be admired only when it costs something. When "hypocrisy" is out of fashion, it costs very little to say, "Well, I'm not a hypocrite. Everybody does the same, but I'm honest enough not to hide it. I don't pretend to be what I'm not."

Real honesty means not only knowing what you are doing and not being ashamed to say so, but knowing *why* you are doing it. Honesty means being willing to face the kind of person you are because you want to act in this particular way. That includes asking whether your real motive is not just self-centeredness—"hardness of heart."

The question Christians must ask is this: Are we willing to recognize God's will for us? And that question follows from asking this: What is God's will for humanity?

DOUBLE STANDARDS

The worst feature of Victorian "hypocrisy" was its double standard. Men were allowed one standard of sexual morals and family morals, and women, a different standard. The double standard often led men to believe that by a "law of nature" there were two kinds of women—"good" women, destined to be wives and mothers; and "bad" or "light" women, who lived to give sexual gratification. Since the second kind of woman was thought to be a breed apart, men considered themselves justified in making use of her. Of course, all such adventures were kept outside the family. As the old drinking toast put it: "To our wives and sweethearts—may they never meet!"

Quite clearly, the explanation that women come in two kinds was an attempt to justify the male double standard. People believed in the sanctity of the home. This belief stemmed partly from the memory of God's declaration that a man "shall cleave unto his wife: and they shall be one flesh" (Genesis 2:24, KJV), and partly from the social and economic importance of the family. This made it important to keep the ideal of the "good woman" clear of all tarnish. An affair after marriage was judged much more serious if it involved a married woman. Before marriage, the important thing was that a man not cause any scandal that would reflect upon the family. But the common view was that, as long as he did not compromise any "nice girl" (the sort that would become a "good woman"), a young male would make a better husband if he had "sown his wild oats" before marriage. The love of a "good woman" would make everything right.

The double standard has not died out, although few would defend it as openly as it used to be defended. Today, some people who think of themselves as supporters of the Sexual Revolution suggest that *both* men and women should experience sexual relations freely until they decide to get married. Then, for the sake of their family, they should settle down with their chosen partner. Some even say that, human nature being what it is, each partner in a marriage should be tolerant of the other's having an occasional short-term affair. Most do not wish to go that far.

The old male double standard was wrong from the point of view of God's will for humanity because it divided the human race. It did so in order to give men greater freedom, of course. Wrong though that was, the basic wrong lay in the fact that marriage and sexuality were put into different compartments of life. Men set up those compartments for their own convenience, and women accepted them, or at least they put up with them. Doing away with the male double standard recognizes that both men and women partake of humanity, and that both have a stake in all that involves their sexual satisfactions and social contracts. But allowing sexual freedom outside marriage does not automatically do away with double standards. Humanity is still divided, but in another direction: before and after marriage.

Human beings cannot direct their lives by one set of standards before marriage and by a totally different set after marriage. Freedom of sexual self-expression and putting the well-being of a family first are totally opposite attitudes toward existence. No one passes from the one to the other without a complete shift in values. To say the least, it is unrealistic to expect such a transformation to take place without a radical and painful self-transformation. That transformation can happen, and it often did long before the so-called Sexual Revolution. But, in the past, there was a whole set of social and religious ideals guiding an individual through that transformation. The "sanctity" of the family was deeply and seriously held by many, and the hypocrisy of the period supported it to a degree. Today it is much harder to keep such an ideal because people believe that the happiness they find (or hope to find) in marriage is what makes it a true marriage. The standard of self-expression, including sexual self-expression, has become second nature; and divorce is the obvious way out when marriage and family seem to be frustrating the self-expression of either partner in a marriage.

LOSING SIGHT OF THE KINGDOM

The Victorians were shocked at the thought of a wife and mother walking out of her husband's home and slamming the door behind her. But what is really shocking is that any person, male or female, should walk out and leave the family to get along without one of its main supports. One of the most serious social problems today is the father leaving his family. This always has been a problem among families at the poverty level, but in our large-scale urban culture the problem has increased enormously. The legal version of walking out, through divorce, causes less economic hardship, but the psychological and the spiritual damage is no less appalling.

The social worker may see the problem economically, in terms of a family unprovided for, or psychologically, in terms of children without the love and care of both parents. But as long as the problem is not seen as a spiritual problem, the roots of the issue remain untouched. Hardness of heart is the continual wound that proves fatal to the community of the family.

Basic to all else is the vision of the wholeness of humanity bound up in the unity of man and woman who, one in heart, become one flesh. When women and men lose sight of God's will for the unity of the human family, marriages are dissolved. Those joined by God have been divided by man. By walking away from God's purpose and "going out" of marriage, a man or a woman has broken the living body of family unity. "Going out" is easy. "Coming in" to the human family and staying there demands vision and purpose—and faith.

TEACHING-LEARNING SUGGESTIONS

Topic Question
How do Jesus' teachings about the kingdom of God apply to the relationship between a man and woman?

Goal
Decide if and why it is important for you to answer the topic question. You may want to reword the question or to write your own. Then, decide what you want to find out in order to answer your question.

Preview of the Lesson
(This outline of the main ideas in the chapter and the related questions are to aid the leader who chooses the lecture-discussion method of teaching.)

1. Ibsen's *A Doll's House* is an early and still powerful statement calling for the recognition of women as persons.
   a. Nora Helmer affirmed her dignity as a person apart from her role as wife and mother.
   b. In striking out of her husband's home, Nora sought to enter or come into a new social relationship with others.
2. Jesus' teachings about the kingdom or rule of God suggest a new and vital relationship with others.
   a. Jesus taught that human life depends on male and female coming together, each as fully human beings.
   b. Jesus linked marriage to the original will of God; marriage is male and female humanity made visible and concrete in the union of husband and wife.
   c. Jesus describes as adultery any separation of the union of husband and wife, for such separation is contrary to God's will for the unity of humanity; it is unfaithfulness to God as well as to the partner.
3. Jesus' teachings represent an ideal made possible not through laws but through repentance and an honest seeking of God's will.
4. In losing sight of the ideal of the kingdom of God, men develop double standards of morality and sexual behavior.
   a. Double standards require the judging and labeling of women as "good" or "bad." Such labeling by men places men in a superior position and rejects the personhood of each woman.
   b. Double standards separate marriage and sexuality; such standards deny that both men and women belong to humanity.
   c. Double standards destroy the unity of humanity.

Related Questions to Discuss
1. How can a woman of today know if she is living in a "doll's house"? Why might some contemporary women

prefer to live in a "doll's house"? What is a woman doing to herself and to her husband by choosing a "doll's house" existence?

2. Can a woman separate her dignity as a person from her dignity as a wife and mother? Explain your answer.

3. If a woman of today chooses to leave her "doll's house," where can she go? How can she come into a new social relationship with others if those "others" remain in the culture she left?

4. In what ways is Jesus' call to men and to women different? In what ways is it alike for both sexes?

5. What is the "new social relationship" to which Jesus called both men and women? Answer in detail.

6. In what ways are husbands and wives unfaithful to the will of God, that is, adulterous, even though no sexual infidelity has taken place? Illustrate with examples.

7. How can a person learn real honesty—the willingness to face the kind of person he is?

8. What advantages did the Victorian double standard have for men? What advantages for women did it provide?

9. In what ways does the double standard continue today?

10. What specific facets of our way of life need to be changed in order to affirm the unity of humanity?

11. For what reasons would you condone divorce? Is divorce always the human-caused division of that which God has joined? Explain your answer.

12. If marriage and the intimate partnership of men and women is the will of God for the unity of humanity, then why do women outnumber men, leaving some persons inevitably unfulfilled?

(The suggestions below are designed to aid leaders and groups desiring a variety of teaching-learning techniques. Choose and adapt those suggestions best suited to the needs of your group.)

Begin

Commence this session by role playing (or discussing) the scene between Nora and Torvald Helmer after Torvald discovered that the danger of the scandal no longer existed. Create your own dialogue spontaneously. You might find the role play more interesting if you put the scene in a contemporary setting. Following the role play, discuss questions such as these: Could Nora have achieved her goals without walking out on Torvald? Could she have made him understand her feelings in some less drastic way? How do women of today protest against the "doll's houses" they live in?

Continue

Spend some time in Bible study: Divide into three teams. Assign team one to study Matthew 5:3-14, then to describe for the group how these verses apply to the relationship between men and women. Team two should examine Luke 20:27-36, then discuss this question before the whole group: What does this passage imply about marriage and about the relationship of men and women? Team three might examine 1 Corinthians 14:34-35, and indicate for the whole group how this passage relates to the teachings of Christ on the unity of men and women. Can you as a whole group agree on a statement describing the Bible's teachings about the relationship of men and women?

Consider in detail how the double standard continues to operate in our society.

". . . the wholeness of humanity bound up in the unity of man and woman . . ." (page 34). Share experiences and illustrations that support or question this idea. What does the statement mean to you?

Conclude

Discuss any insights you have gained thus far toward a possible answer for the question "What does it mean to be a man or to be a woman?"

DAVID STANSBURY

the
man
&the
woman

3

Scripture: **Genesis 1:26-31; 2:18-25**

> **The creation story makes clear that man and woman together are God's crown of creation. The man is not complete without the woman, nor the woman without the man. Together they have a task to do—humanity's task before God.**

In Dorothy Sayer's play *The Zeal of Thy House* a young cherub asks, "Why did God create mankind in two different sorts, if it makes so much trouble?" The Archangels standing by are shocked.

"Hush! you mustn't ask Why," whispers Raphael.

"Angels never ask Why," comments Michael.

"Only men ask Why," adds Gabriel.

Cassiel, the Recording Angel, says severely, "And you see what happened to them, just for asking Why."

Then all the angels shout at the unfortunate cherub: "Criticising God's creation! I never heard of such a thing!" [2]

Men and women, the two sorts of God's creation, keep on asking Why. Young cherubs of the human kind ask very early. But most of the questions children ask about the opposite sex are not *sexual* questions at all. They are questions about the way "the two different sorts" of mankind fit into the human community:

"Why do boys get to have all the fun?"

"Girls get away with anything."

Both boys and girls, early in life, get the impression that the opposite sex has an unfair advantage, at least in certain areas, over their own sex. Yet the fact that few boys wish to be girls, while many girls at times may wish to be boys, shows a male bias in our civilization. Working out a true relationship between the sexes, one that neither denies nor exaggerates the differences between them, is perhaps the basic task facing society today. No society can exist without *some* guidelines for the relationship between the sexes.

PARTNERS IN CREATION

God willed to create man in two different sorts:

> God created man in the image of himself,
> in the image of God he created him,
> male and female he created them. [3]
> (Genesis 1:27, *The Jerusalem Bible*)

The story of Adam and Eve (Genesis, Chapters 2 and 3) expands the first account of creation by saying that God did not consider it good for Adam to be alone. So he created Eve, whom Adam welcomed as his wife.

The account of Eve's being made from Adam's rib seems rather odd until we look at the words with which Adam welcomes her. Adam exclaims:

"This at last is bone of my bones
and flesh of my flesh."
(Genesis 2:23a)

Such an expression was the Hebrew way of saying that a person was dearly loved and counted as one of the family. A parent or a child, a brother or sister, and even cousins had a claim upon those who were, as we say today, "blood relatives." A wife, however, is not in this category. In some societies she has no rights of her own and is useful only if she can bear children for her husband. Adam's exclamation is meant to show that, in God's intention, a wife has full claim upon her husband's affection in her own right and not merely as a potential child-bearer. Our first parents were "one flesh" from the beginning, even before they were sexually united and became parents themselves. So Adam's welcome for Eve expresses the way man and wife are to become "one flesh" in each generation to come (Genesis 2:24).

The word "helpmeet" came into the English language through the King James Version of the Bible. In Genesis 2:18 God proposes to make for Adam "an help meet for him." The New English Bible uses the word "partner" instead of "helpmeet," and the choice is a good one. For *partner* is what the Genesis story implies. Man is created in two different sorts, yet the two together form a partnership.

Sometimes it is thought that, because Adam was created first, the male is the real representative of humanity and the female is an afterthought, a kind of lesser breed who is inferior to the male. This cannot be correct, since Genesis 1:27 shows clearly that man is both male *and* female. First there is a common humanity in which all created persons share. Then there is the existence of partnership, the separate existence of the male and the female, who together can become "one flesh."

41

PARTNERSHIP IS MORE THAN ONE PLUS ONE

The biblical notion of partnership can be used as a standard by which to judge the history of male exploitation of women. This is not to say that the Bible necessarily supports present-day ideas of the equality of the sexes. Partnership and equality are by no means the same.

Partnership depends upon inequality quite as much as upon equality. Recognition of the differences of talent and work are as important as the sharing of common tasks. What matters is that the partnership is a real sharing, not a false one consisting of one person exploiting another, a master lording it over a slave. That is why the black man today does not want simply to be allowed to come quietly into the white man's world. He is insisting that "Black is beautiful." In other words, he is making it clear that partnership exists only when the differences are appreciated.

Partnership at its most basic level is seen in the partnership of man and woman in marriage. Here, one plus one does not make two, but one. Mathematical equality does not apply. As in the kingdom of God, the ruler in the partnership of marriage must be the servant. To be highly exalted is to be lowly. To be free is to be bound.

THE AMERICAN DREAM: MALES WITHOUT FEMALES

The genuine partnership between man and woman that was God's will for mankind has been denied and perverted throughout history. In the modern world, and particularly in the New World of America, it has been perverted in a particular way because of the ideal of equality.

The ideal of equality encourages the individual to think of himself as a separate unit competing with other units. No other unit should be superior, have more, or go further. The rugged "individualism" of the frontier was one expression of this ideal as it developed in America. The individual was confident of his worth and of the opportunities open to him to seek his ideal. The class differences of European society, a society chaining the individual to his inherited position in the scheme of things, had been left behind. America was a new Promised Land, a new Eden awaiting an Adam to till the land and subdue it.

But what about Adam's partner, Eve, in the new Eden? A wife ties a man down, curbs his freedom. Once Adam takes a female partner and accepts the responsibilities of a family man, he is no longer his own master. His relationships bind him to a life of restrictions and compromises very different from his dream of carving an earthly paradise out of the wilderness.

The American dream has been very much a *male* dream. The classic ending of the Western movie portrays the heart of the dream: a lonely Adam on horseback rides into a sunset that carries the promise of a new and glorious tomorrow. In this dream women are troublesome intruders —or sentimental memories. Partnership is understood as temporary cooperation between independent males thrown together when their paths happen to cross. The male partnership may involve affection and inspire loyalty, but it does not create permanent ties.

American authors have written again and again about the American dream of a womanless Eden. One early version is Washington Irving's "Rip Van Winkle." Here the hero is driven from home by his shrewish wife because he will not work to support his family. He sleeps and awakens to discover that his wife is dead and a free America has come into being. For Rip, both pieces of news are equally welcome; and, in the American dream, they are closely connected. Freedom is to be won by refusing to be bound by a female partner; then a man can head into the hills with a dog, a gun, and a keg of liquor. In "Rip Van Winkle," incidentally, all the years that Rip lay sleeping he dreamed he was in male company.

The best-known statements of the American dream are to be found, however, in Mark Twain's *Adventures of Tom Sawyer* and *Adventures of Huckleberry Finn.* These characters have come to be loved and admired in the same way that legendary heroes are loved in other lands. Neither Tom nor Huck knows anything of a family based on the partnership of parents. Like Rip Van Winkle, Tom and Huck find freedom and adventure by escaping the grasp of women who wish to tie them down within a regulated society. When their individual fortunes throw them together, they discover the satisfaction of male partnership.

Huck has a father, but a father who lays on him no bonds he cannot break. His father is the town drunk and an outlaw from traditional society. From him Huck learns to love freedom divorced from responsibilities. The personal code that Huck adopts—a code quite unlike the one that society has taught him—is to be independent and to be loyal to other independent males. Mark Twain suggests (1) that a true male's instincts are far better than the rules of society that sanctify shame and hypocrisy; and (2) that disregarding the woman-taught values of prudence and conformity will make the American male a hero.

The American dream reverses God's statement found in Genesis and says that it *is* good for the man to be alone.

THE MOTHER AND THE GIRL

Mothers have sentimental value for American men. They must be good since they produce male children. As long as they are not curbing male independence, they are to be admired and praised. The most admired mother-figure is the portrait of Whistler's mother, sitting in her chair, serene and dignified by her years. But mothers are also forces to be reckoned with. They are the individuals who, from the days of toilet training, teach males the traditions of society and prepare them for partnership in adulthood. Even when they grow older, they have a habit of getting out of their chairs and laying down female law in terms unwelcome to male ears.

So America, the land of the male dream, invented Mother's Day. But it also invented "Momism"—the legend of the Terrible Female who enslaves her menfolk and smothers their masculine egos in feminine possessiveness.

The Tom Sawyer and Huckleberry Finn stories avoid attacking the mother sentiment directly. Rather, these books use mother substitutes, aunts and widows, who as menless women carry the sole responsibility of disciplining the boys. So Mark Twain seems to be telling us that, no matter how well-meaning they may be, women can never understand males. They try to bind them to rules and to an orderly pattern of society that go against the male instinct for freedom.

At the same time, Adam in the new Eden cannot pretend that Eve was never created. Every male is some mother's son, and after puberty he feels the need for a sexual mate. But, since partnership with woman threatens male independence, the American male has invented classes of women who can be "his" women without making permanent demands upon him. The Mother of Mother's Day is one invention. The Girl is another.

The Girl, even today, is imagined in the two forms of the old male double standard. First of all she is the temporary sex object. While the paid professional Girl (either actual prostitute or the legal substitute used in commercial advertising) may be turned to by men in search of the Girl, she is far from being the ideal Girl. The ideal is the young and beautiful female who gives herself sexually without any reservations simply because of the irresistible maleness of the male. She exists mostly in novels, especially in novels of adventure where the hero is an independent male who is tied to no social conventions. Ian Fleming's spy-thrillers, for example, have been popular largely because his super-hero James Bond, who is licensed to kill, always wins a Girl along with his victory over assorted super-villains. The combination seems to satisfy male fantasy.

Although the Girl is supposed to be sexually available to the true male, she is also innocent and pure. Any other kind of female would be a threat to male independence. She is the opposite of the harlot-figure, the scheming Delilah who betrays her man and makes him her slave or the slave of the society which she represents. Even if the Girl happens to be a prostitute, she is always seen to be basically unsordid, the nice girl next door. For example, the prostitute-heroine of the film *Never on Sunday* challenges, unbelievably but successfully, the underworld bosses, the police, and the American middle-class morality of her would-be American reformer. Her profession is excused as no more than an expression of her freedom from the hypocrisies of society.

If the Mother keeps male admiration by remaining in her chair, the Girl keeps male love by being a fantasy figure promising the delights of sexual conquest without making any demands. She exists in order to make men feel male without having to enter into any real male-female relationships.

Tom Sawyer's school-boy devotion to Becky Thatcher is an early example of the Girl theme in American literature. F. Scott Fitzgerald expresses this theme in *The Great Gatsby*. Like Tom Sawyer, Fitzgerald's hero Jay Gatsby lies nobly in order to protect his Girl from harm, and he feels rewarded simply because he has performed this service for her. Although Gatsby is a gangster and a cheat, he is selfless in his love for Daisy; and he dies thinking that she has never really loved anyone but him. Fitzgerald intends for us to believe that Gatsby's death is a true sacrifice, in spite of—or perhaps because of—the fact that Daisy is no true Girl but a selfish, destructive female.

The Girl is a male ideal; she is not a woman. That is why she is used by advertisers to sell everything from toothpaste to automobiles. Her sole reason for existence is to make males feel that she would be the perfect sexual mate. But she is literally too ideal to touch, whether she poses as the glossy-picture playmate of girlie magazines or walks out on Wall Street in a tight sweater, causing curious businessmen to fill the street to play the game of Girl watching. Real women, however much they may look and act the part of the Girl, are much more complex—and much more demanding. Men's imaginations may invent the Girl and the Mother; God created woman. And woman exists, not to flatter the male ego, but to be female humanity together with but distinct from male humanity.

SOCIETY WITHOUT PARTNERSHIP

Insofar as America has been inspired by Jewish and Christian beliefs, it has understood the family to be the basic unit of society. This understanding has been of utmost importance in American history, and it is still widely influential in spite of the rival view that we have called the American dream. Wherever the biblically based understanding of the family has remained strong, the ideal of partnership between men and women has been kept alive also.

Today, nearly one in every three American marriages ends in the divorce court. Evidently, increasing numbers of people do not think of marriage as a lifelong covenant. They think of it rather as an arrangement that is to last only as long as it is convenient and pleasant. This attitude results in a society with marriage contracts, but without partnership between man and woman.

The American dream of a male society without women has more to do with the breakdown in marriage and family life than might appear on the surface. Huck Finn refused to continue in the care of Aunt Sally because he felt that she wanted to "sivilize" him. The woman is seen as the temptress who will lure the Adam of the new Eden back to the restricted Old World society from which he has escaped. This theme emerges often, even where the goodness of family life seemingly is being upheld. For instance, some popular television series, such as "My Three Sons" and "Bonanza," have shown the ideal family as an all-male household.

"Bonanza," which has remained a favorite for many years, is especially interesting. To begin with, it is set in the new Eden of the American frontier, where men can be free men away from contaminated and contaminating civilization. The father, Ben Cartwright, has a solid, countrified name, recalling the rugged America of Ben Franklin's time. He treats his three sons as an elder brother might. The boys are born of different mothers, for each of Ben Cartwright's wives dies after she has done her duty of bearing him a male child. Providence knew what was best for male happiness and arranged to have the men live in a world without women. Thus the widower can look back fondly, shedding a tear for the loved ones who departed so conveniently. He also sees to it that other women who visit his male reserve do no more than visit. Providence, in any event, continues to watch over his household. Any female who awakens flighty feelings in the breasts of his boys is likely to go at once into a decline and die. In "Bonanza," mothers and girls alike are transformed into sentimental memories instead of remaining to become intruding presences.

The fact that supposedly "family" entertainment teaches an unreal view of womanhood points to one of the causes of family breakdowns. There can be no solution to the problem of the marriage contract and no answer to the question of the roles of man and woman in society until the issue of partnership is faced rather than evaded.

TEACHING-LEARNING SUGGESTIONS

Topic Question
How is our contemporary culture interfering with the partnership between man and woman that God planned in the creation?

Goal
Decide if and why it is important for you to answer the topic question. You may want to reword the question or to write your own. Then, decide what you want to find out in order to answer your question.

Preview of the Lesson
(This outline of the main ideas in the chapter and the related questions are to aid the leader who chooses the lecture-discussion method of teaching.)

1. Society develops guidelines for the relationship between men and women.
   a. Children learn these guidelines as part of their earliest experience.
   b. These guidelines often exaggerate the differences between men and women; thus persons may feel that the other sex has an unfair advantage.
2. But in God's creation, male and female are partners; neither is subservient to the other.
   a. A woman has a claim on her husband's affection apart from her role as a child-bearer because she is a person.
   b. Male and female in partnership comprise the common humanity of God's creation.
3. Partnership has been misunderstood to mean equality.
   a. Equality tends to overlook individual differences.
   b. Partnership is based on inequality.
      1. In a partnership, differences are recognized and appreciated as that which is unique about each person.
      2. In a partnership, two unequals come together to form a single unity; in equality, two equals continue to be two separate but equal units.
4. The idea of equality leads to competition, and this in turn has led to the American dream of "rugged individualism."
   a. Literature illustrates the separateness men feel from women when women try to restrict the male's independence.
   b. American men have created two basic stereotypes of women—the "Mom," a placid, supportive, temporary authority, and the "Girl," a sex object for male needs.
5. The stereotypes created by the American dream deny personhood to both males and females, thus making partnership impossible.

Related Questions to Discuss

1. Why must every society develop guidelines for the relationships between men and women?
2. Do more girls wish to be boys than boys wish to be girls? If your answer is yes, why?
3. In becoming "one flesh" with her husband, does a woman become as close as a blood relative? Or closer? Explain your answer.
4. What is the difference between partnership of male and female and *equality* of male and female?
5. When is the idea of equality not enough? When is partnership more important than equality?
6. How can you learn to appreciate differences between persons?
7. Why does an emphasis on equality result in increased competition? Why does competition result in isolating one from another?
8. What do you understand to be the "American dream" of rugged individualism? What is the role of women in that dream?
9. Is it ever possible for a "rugged individualist" to be in lifelong partnership with a woman? Explain your answer.
10. Why do American men divide women into the stereotypes of "Mom" and "the Girl"? How do women feel about these stereotypes? What do these stereotypes do to women? And to the men who hold the stereotypes?
11. What part does mass entertainment play in fostering the images of the American dream and the stereotypes it includes?

(**The suggestions below are designed to aid leaders and groups desiring a variety of teaching-learning techniques. Choose and adapt those suggestions best suited to the needs of your group.**)

Begin

To begin this session, seat the men in your group in a small circle. Allow the women to sit behind the men in a larger circle surrounding the men. Now, give the men this question to discuss: How did you feel and what thoughts or reactions came to your mind as you read this chapter? After the men have discussed this question for several minutes, let the women ask questions of the men for *clarification only*. The purpose of this exercise is to help the men describe their feelings and to help the women listen carefully to what the men are saying. Or, let two or three men describe for the whole group their thoughts and feelings as they read this chapter.

Continue

Remain in two groups, one consisting of men and the other of women. Working independently, let each group discuss the images of maleness that come through television, motion pictures, and popular novels. Each group should attempt to characterize and describe the "typical American man" as he is presented in our popular culture. Let the groups share their descriptions. Discuss in detail: At what points do men and women agree in their description of our culture's image of the typical man? At what points do they disagree? Why?

As a whole group, list examples or illustrations that support or reject this statement: Cultural images of what men are supposed to be and what women are supposed to be get in the way of an authentic partnership between a man and a woman.

Conclude

End this session by discussing as couples: How is our marriage a partnership? In what ways is it based on the equality concept?

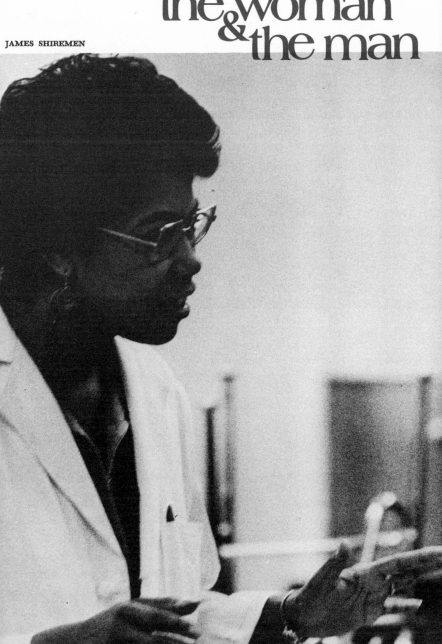

4
the woman & the man

JAMES SHIREMEN

Scripture: Proverbs 31:10-31
The ideal woman of Old Testament times is
pictured as the respected and efficient wife and
mother.

The whole story of civilization, right up to the present, has been a story shaped by males. All nations and groups look back to "praise famous men and our fathers that begat us." (Our mothers must have been there too, for without them none of us would be around to speak about the fathers.) But mothers are very much in the background. Judaism remembers its patriarchs, Christianity its church fathers, the United States its founding fathers, and Canada its fathers of confederation. Painting has its old masters, but no old mistresses. Even science has only Madame Curie on its roll of fame. Hollywood alone remembers both males and females when it recalls its golden age.

The society that we read about in the Bible was very much a patriarchal society. The male dominated, so much so that the size of the nation of Israel was determined by counting adult males only—and adding the words "besides women and children." Until recent times, women had no official place in the worship of the synagogue. We are not surprised, then, to find that when female virtue is praised in the Old Testament, it is taken for granted that the woman's place is in the home.

Nevertheless, the women of the Bible appear as real individuals. Though they generally stand in the shadows of their fathers and husbands, they are full personalities in their own right. Two books of the Old Testament carry the names of women: Ruth and Esther. Both books give accounts of women who, through strength of character, played a part in the history of their people. During the time of the Judges there was even a woman ruler. Deborah the prophetess led the people and claimed for herself the title of "a mother in Israel" (Judges 5:7). Motherhood was a mark of honor among Jewish people. When Deborah claimed that all the people of Israel were her children, she was moved to protect her children and to train them for greatness out of her spirit of motherhood.

In New Testament times the position of women was altered very little. All the Apostles were men. However, we do know the names of the women who were part of the group most closely associated with Jesus—for example, Mary, Martha, and Mary Magdalene. Perhaps it is significant that, as Luke tells us, Jesus was welcomed and blessed in infancy by the old man Simeon and the holy woman Anna (Luke 2:25-38). The Messiah came to save humanity, male and female.

WOMEN IN A MALE WORLD

In a patriarchal society the lives of women were very restricted, but they had a recognized place. If men ruled the nation, women ruled the household. The married woman or "matron" occupied a position of real power and prestige. Because the family rather than the individual was the social unit, the "lord" was not complete without his "lady," whether their home was a castle or a cottage. Legally, the male head of the house was supreme. In fact, it frequently happened that the female "wore the pants," and everyone knew it. In Charles Dickens' *Oliver Twist* the henpecked Mr. Bumble was told that the law supposed that his wife acted under his direction. Mr. Bumble replied: "If the law supposes that, the law is . . . a idiot. If that's the eye of the law, the law is a bachelor; and the worst I wish the law is, that his eye may be opened by experience—by experience." [4]

In a society based on the family the woman stands for the continuity of the family. Thus, the woman has a very clear image of her own role not only as wife and mother but also as teacher of her children—sons as well as daughters—about their future roles as men and as women. When, however, the individual replaces the family as the central unit in a society, male and female roles are no longer clear. What does seem clear is that women are allowed much less opportunity for self-development and self-expression than men, since they are tied to the home in a way that men are not.

The movement for women's rights arose out of the ideas of democracy and equality—ideas men have claimed to support. Yet, a little over one hundred years ago John Stuart Mill wrote his famous essay on "The Subjection of Women." Mill argued that women were prevented from competing with men in public life in order to keep them in the role of servants in the home "because the generality of the male sex cannot yet tolerate the idea of living with an equal." [5]

Most of the legal restrictions that kept women dependent upon men have been removed since Mill's day. Nevertheless, many of the issues raised in "The Subjection of Women" are being discussed today by advocates of Women's Liberation. Mill thought that women could not suddenly become the equals of men, for our whole civilization had been shaped by male supremacy and ingrained attitudes are much harder to change than laws. Attitudes are what Women's Liberation is most concerned about changing now, and this explains why its extreme statements offend at least as many women as men. The movement wishes to create a new self-image for woman, to free her from the understanding of "femininity" that has been current in a male-dominated society (a doll with polished nails, wearing satins and laces, and smelling of cologne), for passive acceptance of this understanding has hurt women. Slavery, so the argument goes, can be overcome only when its victims revolt.

Insofar as women have little idea of what their role in society should be, Women's Liberation makes a valid point. Lacking a clear self-image, the woman in modern society will reflect the image coming through the mass media, the image of the Girl of the male dream. And by doing so, woman will be kept from achieving true humanity.

The bra-burning incident is one of the most publicized and most ridiculed actions of the women's movement. It may not have been the most effective means to its intended end, but it made some sense. The extreme concentration of interest upon female breasts is a modern American phenomenon; it had no parallel in Europe before the spread of American culture to the Old World. A prominent bosom is the symbol of the Girl, the male's playmate, because it emphasizes the "play" aspect of sex rather than the procreative aspect. Certainly, female acceptance of this male image keeps it in fashion; and a protest aimed at destroying a stereotype and allowing women some natural dignity as human beings is a good thing.

At the same time, bra-burning and all similar demonstrations are misguided if their main object is to express female hostility toward the male, or toward women's dress as an expression of sexuality. Protests should be directed instead toward the exploitation of women's sexuality.

WOMAN'S IMAGE OF HERSELF

Women's Liberation is correct in complaining that woman has allowed her self-image to be made for her by a male-dominated society. From the billboard, magazine cover, and television screen we are bombarded with images of the Girl. Women are persuaded that they can keep their self-respect and win attention and envy only if they conform to this image. So the American wife is told to be the thirty-year-old who cannot be detected among a crowd of teenagers. The American mother is told her hair and skin can match those of her daughter. And this propaganda works; if it did not, advertisers would not waste their money on the effort.

Mothers pass on the Girl image to their daughters. In one of his short stories, J. D. Salinger describes a beach scene in which a small girl, playing beside her fashionable mother, is wearing a yellow two-piece swimming suit. Obviously the child would not be needing one piece of that suit for another nine or ten years.[6] Here Salinger observes that the child is not allowed to be a child. Because she is a female, she is being paraded already in the image of the Girl. Many mothers *do* understand that their children are young human beings first of all, and male or female in the second place. But some mothers make far too much difference between their boy children and their girl children. They give boys a freedom that they deny to girls, expecting their daughters, as a matter of course, to take over the responsibilities in the home while their sons go out "with the boys." While their daughters are still in their early teens, mothers fret openly about their daughters' chances of getting married. And so they pass on the idea that a woman finds her happiness only in dependence upon a man.

A child who grows up hoping that she will be some man's Girl has a false image of the male in her mind. She is bound to be disillusioned, for her image of marriage is far from the real situation in which two human beings have to learn to live together and to master the physically and emotionally exhausting business of bringing up a family. The imagined husband of the Girl is someone who is constantly attentive, generous, and sexually ardent. He is attractive to other women; but he can love only the one he has chosen to be *his*, since love is the only true basis for marriage. If they have children, he will be a big brother to his sons, and she will be an understanding older sister to her daughters.

While the image of the Girl remains popular, it is no wonder divorce is so common. Neither is it surprising that, while desertion of families by fathers is still the most common social pattern, cases of mothers who leave husband and children are increasing very rapidly. Women simply are discovering that they are not prepared to bear the demands made on them by marriage, demands that are not included in their image of life with a man. Love based upon sexual attraction may widen into the kind of love that endures through all the problems aging partners experience. But it is not likely to do so when the husband thinks of his wife as the Girl who exists chiefly to show off his maleness and when the wife thinks of her husband as the lover whose chief concern is to make her feel that she is his Girl.

When the ideal of motherhood remained strong, women did not easily desert the home. But, for a good many years now, the Mother image has been treated with disfavor while the Girl image (with its ideal of sexual fulfillment) has become more popular than ever. So the old joke about the wife packing her clothes and running home to mother has a new and much more serious dimension. The disappointed wife, who may also be a mother, runs away— away from home life as such—in order to find a life where she can be herself.

If we look at the way modern films deal with the problems of men and women, we can see how often running away is the prescription for living. Seldom are there indications that any more positive or permanent solution is possible. In the film *Easy Rider* the American dream of the free male unencumbered by females (except as passing relaxation) lives again. Motorcycles have replaced the horse, but civilization is still the enemy. Settled communities with their traditional values are seen as the breeding ground of corruption from which envy and hatred reach out to destroy the free-spirited individual in his youth and male potency. The enormously popular film *The Graduate* singles out the Older Woman as the embodiment of the evil of civilized society. Here the young hero finds himself being drawn into the net of hypocritical conformity, represented by his relationship with Mrs. Robinson. He rebels and fights the whole Establishment to win his Girl before she too is captured in a society marriage. The happy ending of the film depends, of course, upon our ignoring the fact that the hero's Girl will presumably grow into an Older Woman with many of the same problems her mother had. Will the younger generation "Mrs. Robinson" then go around corrupting other young Graduates? Nothing in the story suggests a different possibility. While *The Graduate* reflects the atmosphere of the active sixties, the more recent and equally popular film *Love Story* echoes the gentler tone of the "make-love-not-war" generation of the seventies. The story avoids any social problems by having the Boy-and-Girl romance remain wholly in post-adolescence through the time-honored means of having the Girl die before she can become the trouble-making Older Woman. Running away from life into death is, after all, the only certain way of preserving an image of love that does not meet the demands of real life.

BREAKING FALSE IMAGES

The current stereotyped images of masculinity and femininity have been created largely by men. It is natural enough that women should be influenced by men and that they often try to conform to the male image of the female. Women have not been the image-makers, and for that very reason, they are also not as easily taken in by them as men are.

Women are more practical-minded than men. That fact is widely admitted. They seem to be less impressed by abstract ideas. They are more concerned for people than for causes. They prefer supporting specific proven programs rather than arguing about political philosophies. This often is taken to mean that women are less "intellectual" than men. Actually, brain power is not the issue here. Common sense is. Women may well have a very realistic grasp of political life, for the family is the basic political unit; and women have always been the hub of the family. Women know that politics is "the art of the possible" and that ideologies generally stand in the way of workable political decisions. It is interesting to note that today, although relatively few women have succeeded in breaking into national politics, women have been elected to head three of the world's crisis-ridden countries: Israel, India, and Ceylon.

False images prevent us from seeing and dealing with the true situation that lies behind the images. How a woman's practical concern for individuals can break through the screen of false images is well illustrated in Arthur Miller's play *Death of a Salesman*. Willy Loman, the salesman, is a self-deluded man, unable to distinguish between reality and the obsessions that have come to dominate his life. Because his two sons have false images of their father, they do not understand how to help him. But his wife, Linda, a very ordinary woman who has had a hard and unrewarding life with Willy, does understand. She says to the boys:

> I don't say he's a great man. Willy Loman never made a lot of money. His name was never in the paper. He's not the finest character that ever lived. But he's a human being, and a terrible thing is happening to him. So attention must be paid. He's not to be allowed to fall into his grave like an old dog. Attention, attention must be finally paid to such a person.[7]

Knowing when *attention must be paid to a human being* is the knowledge that really counts in human life, and gaining this knowledge means breaking false images— including false images of masculinity and femininity. The image of the Girl hides the real woman who, as a human being, is more than a sexual object, and so prevents true partnership in marriage. Until the Girl image is broken, men will continue to think of women as having no part in the male world except as ornaments and playthings; and women who accept this image will have no reason to be mature human beings and therefore will have no respect for their own role in life.

Not all women are enthusiastic about Women's Liberation. Advocates of the movement say it is because those women have accepted the male image of woman as inferior. But women's distrust of *all* generalized images may be an equally important factor in this lack of enthusiasm. Women who find genuine fulfillment in the roles of homemaker and mother do not agree that they are house-bound slaves who are sacrificing their freedom to male egotism. For them, a theory about sexual equality is not nearly as important as the satisfaction they find in being persons who have an essential service to perform for other persons, a unique service with unique rewards.

This does not mean that there are no inequalities between the sexes that need to be removed. Nor does it mean that all women will find full expression of their talents in looking after a man's well-being and in providing a home for him and the children. If there is to be genuine partnership between men and women, such a partnership cannot be limited to the home. It must find expression also in the larger world of human affairs.

WOMAN ON HER OWN

In the patriarchal societies of the past, male and female roles were clearly defined; and each sex was guaranteed certain satisfactions through doing its own kind of work well. But patriarchal society also fostered the belief that a woman was not meant for "man's work." That is, she was unsuited because of her physical nature and not simply because society favored men working in the community at large and women working in the home. This belief implies also that only the women who are sexually unattractive ought to follow a career which requires intelligence and in which feminine charm is not an asset.

Theoretically, a woman may be free to engage in work for which she feels suited; yet she finds it hard to follow a career on her own, as a person possessing certain abilities in her own right and independent of her sex. If she marries, she may feel that she must give time to bearing and bringing up children and to supporting her husband in his career rather than pursuing a career of her own. When this is her choice, she will probably consider the compromise well worth while. And she may find opportunity to take up her own work again when her children no longer require a mother's constant attention. Nevertheless, the fact remains that her life is restricted by her sex to a much greater extent than a man's life is restricted by family responsibilities. If she does not marry, she finds it very hard to retain full self-respect. In the eyes of most men and of other married women, she has failed as a woman; and her career is second best, a substitute for a truly "feminine" life. And it requires a great deal of courage for her not to accept the image that others may have of her as her own self-image. A bachelor who is married to his work does not create a negative image, but the single woman is labeled "a frustrated female."

The movement for women's rights (which preceded Women's Liberation) fought a long battle to defeat such prejudice. The movement stressed sexual equality. It had to prove that woman is not inferior to man in handling large responsibilities or small ones and that she is not less intelligent, less competent, or less adaptable. When women entered field after field of activity previously thought to be for men only, the myth of female inferiority was broken. Though broken, it has not yet been banished. Women still feel that they are tolerated, rather than accepted, in a man's world.

Sexual equality, in an abstract sense, is not really the solution for the problem of man-woman relationships. What is necessary above all is that both men and women are respected as human beings, in society at large and in the home.

Most of the pioneers in women's rights had to struggle to make their mark in the world outside the family, and this meant giving up family life in order to achieve their goal of professional equality with men. Only occasionally could a woman have both marriage and a career, and usually only when husband and wife shared identical interests. The Curies, for example, were both scientists engaged in the same line of research. Men have always assumed as a matter of course that they can have both a full family life and a career. Even today few women can assume that this is true for them.

A woman with a career finds that her sex is constantly brought into the picture. An extremely common example of this is found in an account of an interview with a woman scientist; it begins something like this: "Sylvia Smith is a smart brunette who looks as though she would be more at home in a Paris fashion house than in a laboratory."

The implication here is that a good-looking woman is wasted in work that does not exploit her looks and direct them to some "feminine" end. The question of women's rights goes far beyond laws giving women equal opportunities to compete with men in the labor market, and involves the attitudes of men toward women and of women toward themselves. The woman in the home needs to know that she is considered to be more than a machine for keeping a house in order and for keeping the children fed, washed, and quiet. She is more than a hostess or an ornament to be displayed around the house. The woman at work needs to know that she is respected for her competence and skills, and not thought of as someone who "never made it" as a woman. The Girl image and the Mother image are the truly destructive symbols of male attitudes of superiority because they deny to all women the consideration to which she is entitled as a human being.

TEACHING-LEARNING SUGGESTIONS

Topic Question
How can the false role images that deny men and women their full humanity be broken so that each individual can have a sense of worth?

Goal
Decide if and why it is important for you to answer the topic question. You may want to reword the question or to write your own. Then, decide what you want to find out in order to answer your question.

Preview of the Lesson
(This outline of the main ideas in the chapter and the related questions are to aid the leader who chooses the lecture-discussion method of teaching.)

1. Throughout history, society has been primarily male-dominated.
   a. Women have usually been defined by place—their position in relationship to their men—and by function—as mothers and maintainers of the home.
   b. Historically, the woman represents the continuity of the family in those cultures built on families.
      (1) Women interpret for sons and daughters the roles they are expected to fulfill as men and women.
      (2) But these roles become extremely confused when

the culture begins to place more emphasis on the individual than on the family.
2. The current interest in new rights for women is a reflection of an emphasis on persons as individuals, not functions.
3. Because they are caught in a time of change, today's women have an unclear self-image.
   a. On one hand, women strive for a sense of being whole persons.
   b. On the other hand, they seek to fulfill the stereotypes of womenhood provided by their mothers and by the popular culture. These male-created stereotypes meet male needs.
4. When a woman seeks to fulfill a stereotype image, she begins to stereotype men and other women as well.
   a. This stereotyping of each sex by the other denies both persons in a relationship their true humanity.
   b. Stereotyping of each sex by the other leads to incompletely fulfilled images within the marriage; divorce is often the result.
5. False images and stereotypes can be broken only when both sexes will risk seeing each other as persons and as individuals.

Related Questions to Discuss

1. Why, historically, has the male been the more dominant sex? What caused men to gain authority over women in the beginnings of civilization, and to retain that authority over the centuries?
2. How does "place" define and limit a person? Reflect on the statement "A woman's place is in the home." If you reject this statement, then what is the "place" of women? And of men?
3. In what ways might a woman "wear the pants" in the family, even though she is economically dependent on her husband? Supply illustrations with your answer.
4. How can a woman come to discover her true humanity in a culture that bombards her with conflicting images of what she should be?
5. What means does an individual woman have at her disposal to challenge and overcome the stereotypes by which she is treated?
6. Where do little girls learn what it means to be women? Where did you learn the meaning of womanhood?
7. In what ways has your understanding of maleness and femaleness changed over the years? What images learned in your childhood do you retain? Why?
8. How can a woman discover a self-identity apart from the images of "Mom" or "the Girl"?
9. What are the sources of mental images of the ideal mate?
10. In what ways is civilization the enemy of a woman seeking

a sense of wholeness and of personhood? Give examples.
11. How do you discover and pay attention to the unique person each individual is? What does "respect for the other" mean?

(The suggestions below are designed to aid leaders and groups desiring a variety of teaching-learning techniques. Choose and adapt those suggestions best suited to the needs of your group.)
Begin

To begin this session, seat the women in your group in a small circle. Allow the men to sit behind the women in a large circle surrounding the women. Now, give the women this question to discuss: How did you feel and what thoughts and reactions came to your mind as you read this chapter? After the women have discussed this question for several minutes, let the men ask questions of the women for *clarification only*. The purpose of this exercise is to help the women describe their feelings and to help the men listen carefully to what the women are saying. Or, let two or three women describe for the whole group their thoughts and feelings as they read this chapter.

Continue

Spend some time at this session sharing experiences. Let several persons describe situations in which they felt they were treated as a stereotype rather than as a person. OR situations in which they tried to break out of the typical roles of men or women. OR situations in which they felt themselves guilty of fostering stereotypes in their children. Do not evaluate or judge another person's experience or his reaction to an experience, but listen for insights that shed light on your own situation. As a result of sharing experiences, can you as a whole group list factors in our society that need to be changed in order to break the stereotypes that deny individuals their personhood?

Let the women in your group deal with this question: What do you say when a friend says, "But I like being a housewife. There's nothing else I want to do. Should I want more?"

Conclude

To close this session, reread Proverbs 31:10-31. Is this picture of woman consistent with what you understand to be the will of God? What, if anything, is missing from this picture?

5
fallen
society

EO M. JOHNSON

E. HOUSTON ST.

BOWER

Scripture: Genesis 3:1-21
> The story of the Fall tells of the breaking of relationships, first between man and God, then between man and woman, and finally between man and the world. Sexuality becomes a problem, and the world that was created good becomes a place of sorrow.

(1) A husband quarrels with his wife and leaves the room in a rage. He goes over it in his mind: "She asks my opinion, so I give it. She starts crying and says I don't love her or I wouldn't be so cruel to her. I tell her to be reasonable. I could easily have lied and said what she wanted to hear, but can't two grown people discuss things like adults even if they disagree? Then she flies into a temper and calls me names. I say that I've had enough. Women take everything personally—at least *I* keep a hold on myself. But I don't have to put up with her tantrums."

(2) A wife looks at her husband across the breakfast table and thinks these thoughts: "Is this the man I

married ten years ago? He hardly seems to notice me unless he wants something done for him. He complains, of course. I'm part of the furniture as far as he's concerned. He wants to take out his spite on me when he's being done in. It's the same, morning after morning, evening after evening. I don't know how much more I can stand."

These two scenes are common ones. The situations shown can go on repeating themselves without any drastic results. The persons involved may get over their resentments, come to some understanding perhaps, or simply decide to go on living together somehow without forcing any parting of the ways. However, a real crisis may come sooner or later, and bottled-up feelings can explode, dangerously and with drastic results. Either of the two incidents might be the beginning of a broken home. They might result in the breaking off of personal relationships for a whole lifetime.

A FALLEN WORLD

All the quarrels, misunderstandings, bitternesses, and hostilities that divide us in the home point to the fact that we live in a fallen world. The same divisions exist between members of larger groups: neighborhoods, ethnic groups, workers and employers, races, nations, blocks of nations. Everyone wants peace and brotherhood, but no one knows how to reach these blessings. Every way tried by men has led to bloodshed and hatred, and the goal remains as distant as ever.

The story of Adam and Eve tells how mankind rejected the right relationship with God for which man was created, and how the evils that we know resulted from that disobedience to the law of man's creation. God's words to Adam and Eve as they were being turned out of Eden describe for us the nature of the fallen world in which we still live.

Dietrich Bonhoeffer, the German theologian and church leader who was killed by the Nazis near the end of the Second World War, has written his interpretation of the meaning of the Fall in his book *Creation and Fall*. He says, "The new things that the tree of knowledge brought upon Adam and Eve are shame and passion." [8]

In the story of the Fall shame and passion are shown taking over the life of Adam and Eve. Adam and Eve knew they were guilty, and so they hid from God. When he called them to him they could not admit their guilt openly and ask for forgiveness. They were ashamed, yet they tried to pretend they were not really to blame. The man blamed the woman; the woman blamed the snake. Also, for the first time they were ashamed of their sexuality revealed in nakedness. Faced with the limits now recognizable in themselves, each wanted to possess the other, thereby denying personhood to the other. This desire to possess another we call passion. Before they left the Garden, God told them what their lives would be like since they had upset his good will for mankind:

> To the woman he said,
> "I will greatly multiply your pain in
>   childbearing;
>   in pain you shall bring forth
>   children,
> yet your desire shall be for your
>   husband,
>   and he shall rule over you."

And to Adam he said,
"Because you have listened to the
    voice of your wife,
  and have eaten of the tree
of which I commanded you,
   'You shall not eat of it,'
cursed is the ground because of you;
   in toil you shall eat of it all the
     days of your life. . . ."
(Genesis 3:16-17)

Sometimes the words of Genesis have been misinterpreted and misused. For instance, they were used against medical men who tried to introduce methods of painless childbirth. God, it was said, had decreed that childbirth should be painful. With the same kind of reasoning, persons have argued that God decreed that man should always be woman's master; therefore, the emancipation of women was contrary to God's law.

Clearly, the Bible is not giving God's will for mankind in this part of the story. Quite the contrary. *The Bible is giving a realistic picture of what human life becomes when God's laws for his creation are disobeyed.* Once the right relationship with God is broken, then all other relationships suffer disorder. Because women bear children, they are vulnerable to men. Through most of the world's history, instead of being men's partners, they have been treated as slaves or considered pieces of property owned by men. God's words to Adam have proven accurate also. For the great mass of mankind, in the past and even today, work has been a struggle for existence—a struggle that is wearing, wearisome, and monotonous rather than rewarding. And over all the achievements of the human race hang the solemn words of God: "You are dust, and to dust you shall return" (Genesis 3:19).

MAN THE TYRANT

At creation God put man—male and female—in charge of the rest of created nature (Genesis 1:28). As long as man lived in obedience to his Creator, the gift of power to "subdue" nature would not be misused. But fallen man does not look upon the power he has been given as a gift; rather he sees it as a right and a license for any and every selfish misuse of power.

Only recently has man's conscience begun to trouble him about his misuse of the physical world around him. Now we are awakening to the frightening fact that we may have already so mistreated our environment that the damage cannot be repaired; we see now that we may have made the earth uninhabitable for our children or our children's children. In this regard, we are learning the truth of the biblical teaching: "Do not be deceived; God is not mocked, for whatever a man sows, that he will also reap" (Galatians 6:7).

On the physical level, then, we are becoming aware that the earth is the Lord's; we cannot ignore his laws indefinitely without having to face the consequences. This lesson may be harder to learn in the area of human relationships. Here also clear danger signals are coming through. As our cities become increasingly difficult to manage as centers of civilized life, we are being forced to acknowledge our sins against human brotherhood. The increases in urban crime and mental illness alarm us and cause us to ask whether we can continue our present social organization of human life.

While good organization is essential, even more essential is our will to be a community. The end of the institution of slavery did not mean the end of the white man's oppression of the black man. And legislation alone, however enlightened, will not bring about a community where black and white can live as brothers.

The basic problem that we face in becoming a community is that fallen man does not want to be a brother, or a partner. He prefers to be a tyrant. He prefers to exploit the world and the people around him for his own selfish ends rather than to work for the common good. The kingdom of self-gratification, and not the kingdom of God, is what he seeks first.

The word "tyrant" calls to mind a picture of a strong and ruthless ruler having power over millions: a Genghis Khan, a Hitler, a Stalin. But the tyrant is found at every level of society and wherever people come into contact with other people. An employer may be a tyrant to his employees, a husband and father a tyrant in his home. Moreover, the tyrant may work through weakness as well as through strength. An invalid can rule a household from a bed, and the youngest child in a family can tyrannize his brothers and sisters unless he is given everything he wants.

Even fallen man, however, has some will toward building a just society. At some stage the tyrant is seen for what he is, and his victims revolt against his rule. But here the nature of fallen man is revealed for what *it* is. Fallen man's idea of liberty may be, in theory, liberty for all men. In practice it is likely to be understood as *liberty for me—and for others to the extent that I'm not inconvenienced.* Thus the overthrow of one tyrant usually means that in a short time another tyrant takes his place.

SHARING AND SACRIFICE

The tyrant is a lonely figure. He cannot tolerate anyone near him who might challenge his power, so he is prepared to sacrifice everyone else in order to keep his position. He can trust no one; so he can love no one. The Roman Emperor Nero once said that he wished all his subjects had only one neck among them so that he could cut off their heads with a single stroke of the sword if need be. That is the hidden wish of every tyrant who rules by fear.

Jesus is the very opposite of the tyrant, as we see in the words of a hymn:

Conquering kings their titles take
  From the foes they captive make;
Jesus, by a nobler deed,
  From the thousands He has freed.[9]

He taught that those who would be counted the greatest in the kingdom of Heaven were those who humbled themselves (Matthew 18:4). Unlike worldly kingdoms, in God's kingdom true rule was found in service: " 'the Son of Man came not to be served but to serve, and to give his life as a ransom for many' " (Matthew 20:28).

Sharing and self-sacrifice are the marks of the community intended by the Creator for his creation. In the family this law of creation is never completely forgotten. The worst of parents make some sacrifices for their children. The least loving of husbands and wives occasionally put themselves out to please their partners.

The marks of fallen creation are seen in family relationships in the small extent to which sharing and sacrifice are put at the center of life. How often a husband or a parent is surprised that providing for wife or child does not result in love being returned. "She had all she asked for, and then she wasn't happy." "I worked to give him the best possible start in life, and I get no thanks." These remarks are heard again and again. But giving things, even at personal sacrifice, can mean very little if the person who receives them thinks the gifts are doled out as a sort of investment to yield a dividend. Such gifts are the bribery of a tyrant, a down payment to buy loyalty—made with an eye to self-interest and in the belief that everyone has his price.

Even self-sacrifice can be selfish if it looks for recognition or is intended to put another person under a debt of obligation. A mother who slaves for her family may do so in order to keep her husband and children dependent upon her, even though she imagines she is being a "real mother" and is showing how much she loves them. Unconsciously, she may be wishing to make them unable to do without her, resenting any signs they show of having a life of their own apart from her.

Sacrifice goes together with sharing. And sharing means that no individual tries to do anything alone. Respect for a person's *otherness* opens the way for truly sacrificial love, a love that wishes other people to be themselves. Such willingness to share points the way out of fallen creation into the community that Jesus called the kingdom of heaven.

COUNTING THE COST

Sharing and sacrifice are costly items on the bill of life. We must be willing to pay for them. "Go now, pay later" is a familiar slogan in our day. Yet Jesus said, "Which of you, desiring to build a tower, does not first sit down and count the cost, whether he has enough to complete it?" (Luke 14:28) Jesus made this comment when he was speaking about the cost of becoming a disciple. He never tried to hide the extent of the cost. "If any man would come after me, let him deny himself and take up his cross and follow me" (Matthew 16:24).

In many quarters today self-denial is considered a life-style that went out with Puritanism. Not just the slogan quoted above but the advertising industry as a whole goes against the idea of self-denial. Advertising is based on the belief that people will buy what they want badly. The advertiser's job is to make them conscious of wants they never knew they had. People are promised quick and easy ways of becoming beautiful, keeping young, keeping free from worry and pain, gaining extra leisure, and being attractive to the other sex or stirring envy in the minds of those of their own sex—all the wants of persons following the path of instant self-fulfillment. Men and women are persuaded that they cannot wait to sample all the pleasant things of life. How much they will have to pay for their impatience and how long they will have to pay are matters they are not expected to think about. The invitation is to self-indulgence without counting the cost.

The invitation seems to be widely accepted. And the blame cannot simply be laid upon the "materialism" of middle-class society. Self-indulgence is just as evident in the so-called counter-culture. Jerry Rubin, a spokesman for the youth revolution, has written a book entitled *Do It.* The activities he praises are very different from those promoted by Madison Avenue. Yet the underlying philosophy is the same: self-expression without thought of the cost.

Increasingly, the "hip" and the "square" world agree in seeing sex as the chief means of finding ourselves as persons. Sex is "liberating" and "creative." To deprive ourselves here is to fail to be full human beings, to make life ugly, and to fill ourselves with frustrations and inhibitions.

If, however, the cost of human sexuality is considered first, the philosophy of "do it" or "go now" looks far less realistic and attractive. Sex always affects more than one individual. In the first place, it brings together two people and unites them in an intimate bond that can never be broken without pain and sorrow. Then, it makes possible the existence of new lives. The men and women of tomorrow—and so the whole human community—are affected by the manner in which their parents have handled their sexuality. The cost of human sexuality is that men and women have to deny themselves in order that the next generation will have the necessary love and care to grow to maturity.

When our desire to get something we want without counting the cost has cost both ourselves and others too dearly, then we will understand what the Bible means when it speaks of the need for repentance.

LAW AND LOVE

The kingdom of heaven into which Jesus called men was a kingdom to be found through repentance. In biblical terms, it was a kingdom whose citizens were forgiven sinners. The Kingdom was God's answer to the plight of a fallen creation.

We too easily forget this. The need for repentance is forgotten in the popular claim that love is the answer to all our problems. Of course, love is the ultimate answer to human problems, since God is love. Yet love is not something we can simply decide to try out, as we can try out a new pair of shoes. We cannot live according to love in the same way we can start to live on a special diet.

Why? The Bible reminds us that love is the fulfilling of the law (Romans 13:10). The Bible tells us also that no one except Jesus has ever lived without sinning against God's law (Romans 3:10; Hebrews 4:15). Even those who are redeemed by grace, being reborn by water and by the Spirit (John 3:5), still carry with them many of the habits and ways of thinking that belong to the unredeemed life. They are not yet "made perfect" in love. John Wesley, who believed that through the Spirit Christians can be led to "Christian perfection," limited that perfection to their having no *conscious* inclination to sin. He never imagined that in this present life we could actually live without breaking God's laws for humanity.

A life of sharing and sacrifice, then, is something we can partly know and follow in love, yet only partly. Because our hearts are never perfectly "right with God," and because our fallen nature is always with us, we cannot simply follow our hearts and thus love our neighbor as ourselves. We need law—human law as well as divine law—to keep us within bounds when our self-will takes command of us and to restrain the actions of shame and passion that are the heritage of mankind's fall into broken relationships.

If we ignore the character of our fallen world we can never begin to find the way back to the humanity that God intended for us. Today Christians as well as non-Christians are prone to overestimate their ability to live under the inspiration of the power of love and to minimize the importance of law to bring about moral behavior.

Recognizing the damage that environmental pollution has done to our world is very far from solving the evils of pollution. Obviously it is not enough to say, "From now on we know what to do, and things are going to be different. Pollution is suicidal; therefore, with some good will all around, pollution will end." We are well aware that good will is likely to make precious little difference if there is not also wise and strict legislation.

The same is true of human relationships. We cannot legislate love of neighbor, but we can keep people from hurting their neighbors in specific ways through right legislation properly enforced.

TEACHING-LEARNING SUGGESTIONS

Topic Question
How is the condition of the fallen world lived out in human relationships?

Goal
Decide if and why it is important for you to answer the topic question. You may want to reword the question or to write your own. Then, decide what you want to find out in order to answer your question.

Preview of the Lesson
(This outline of the main ideas in the chapter and the related questions are to aid the leader who chooses the lecture-discussion method of teaching.)
  1. The hostilities that divide us indicate that we live in a fallen world.
  2. Man has rejected the right relationship with God, and this lack of right relationship with God makes right relationship with self and others difficult, if not impossible.
  3. The fallen world is marked by shame and passion, as indicated in the biblical stories of Adam and Eve.
     a. Shame is a recognition of guilt but a lack of strength to admit the wrongdoing and to seek forgiveness.
     b. Passion is the attempt to possess and exploit another for selfish ends.
  4. God's curse upon Adam and Eve after their fall is not a description of God's will for mankind but a realistic picture of what human life is like after the fall.
  5. In order to come again into a right relationship with God,

man needs a will to community; increased social organization and more developed levels of civilization will not
suffice.

    a. The will to community involves conscious and active
       partnership with others.

    b. Man prefers to be a tyrant, that is, exploitative and
       totally self-centered, rather than a brother and partner.

6. Jesus shows the way toward community.

    a. The tyrant dominates in a variety of ways; Jesus shows
       the way to service and sacrifice as partnership.

    b. The tyrant categorizes and stereotypes all others; Jesus
       teaches respect for each person's *otherness*.

7. The way of Christ involves a cost; it involves a surrender
of personal freedom and "rugged individualism" in order
that full partnership might come about.

8. Laws may help control self-will when it is tempted to
become a tyrant, but only self-giving love can result in
true partnership and a restored relationship with God
and others.

Related Questions to Discuss

1. What is man's right relationship to God? Is it possible to
know this right relationship in a fallen world? Explain
your answer.

2. How do you understand shame and passion? Are shame
and passion always negative qualities? If your answer is *no*,
cite examples to support your answer.

3. Is it against God's will (Genesis 3:14-19) to seek relief
from the pain of childbirth or to employ labor-saving
devices? Support your answer with reasons.

4. In what ways is the current interest in television and
motion picture sex and violence a reflection of the shame
and passion of the fallen world?

5. How can persons gain the will to community? What pro-
hibits persons from expressing their will to community?

6. In what ways do persons tyrannize others? Answer this
question by citing a variety of examples, including the
subtle ways husbands and wives tyrannize one another.

7. What is the difference between the way of Christ and the
way of the tyrant? Spell out this difference in detail.

8. How can a man will for community and share in a partnership without relinquishing his freedom and denying himself? How can a woman do so?

**(The suggestions below are designed to aid leaders and groups
desiring a variety of teaching-learning techniques. Choose and
adapt those suggestions best suited to the needs of your group.)
Begin**

To commence this session, invite the members of the group
to quickly scan this chapter, calling out sentences or phrases

from the chapter that raise questions or comments in their minds. List these sentences or phrases on newsprint or chalkboard. As a whole group, examine and discuss the sentences that have been posted. What central ideas need to be more clearly understood? Does the study book assume a basic stance that some members of the group will not accept? Or is the phrasing and wording of these sentences simply difficult to comprehend? Can you, as a group, resolve the confusion or questions about the sentences you've listed?

Continue

Focus on the idea of fallen persons in a fallen society. In small groups, deal with questions such as these: What does it mean to be fallen? Does the individual always know that he is fallen? What is a fallen man? A fallen woman? Do men experience fallenness differently from women? How? Share insights from the small group discussions with the whole group.

A fallen person is a tyrant; he exploits the world for his own ends. Share illustrations drawn from your own experience of the ways persons tyrannize others. Is a person always aware that he is a tyrant? How can he be helped to see that he is tyrannizing another?

Read Genesis 3:1-21 in several translations of the Bible, then ask your pastor or a similarly qualified person to describe for you the effect this passage has had on the doctrine of sin and other theological ideas throughout Christian history.

Conclude

Using insights from this chapter and your discussion of the ideas in it, describe how you might resolve the two conflict situations outlined at the beginning of this chapter.

6
the
fallen
person

Scripture: Romans 1:18-32
> Paul describes the evil consequences of the
> denial of God's rule in the world.

In a game familiar to most school children, players take turns being famous people in history or in the news, and they ask the other players "Who am I?" Many persons today are asking the same question, but not in a game. The search for identity is one of the big problems of our time.

Every child has to discover his or her identity; it is a part of the process of growing up. At first we are simply the children of our parents, with little to call our own. Gradually other people begin to recognize us as distinct personalities. But since we cannot see ourselves from the outside, we come to think of ourselves mostly in terms of the place we occupy in the family. Discovering who we are, in ourselves and not merely in relation to our elders, takes a long time.

We start life with only one possession that is wholly our own. Suppose you are told that your neighbors down the street have a new baby. Immediately you will ask: "Boy or girl?" You can be sure that question has been asked by everyone who has heard about the event—and first of all, of course, by the baby's mother and father. From the beginning, each individual is a self because of having a particular sex.

Yet this distinguishing mark that makes such a difference when we are born becomes less and less helpful in identifying ourselves as persons as we grow up.

The confusion about identity is a reminder that everyone in the world is, in biblical terms, a fallen person. We have fallen from our created state individually as well as corporately.

THE IDENTITY CRISIS

Because the identity crisis is so much a part of present-day discussion, we sometimes forget it is not entirely new. We cannot know who we are until we have made something of ourselves that distinguishes us from other people; every individual in the world has had to do this. The task is always hard, and it is never finished. For, while the most crucial years for self-discovery are the years from adolescence to adulthood, in a sense we continue to discover who we are with each crisis we meet. As long as we are alive we continue finding unexpected strengths and weaknesses in ourselves that alter the picture of who we are. Indeed, self-discovery does not stop until the end of our lives. When Moses was called by God he said: "Who am I that I should go to Pharaoh, and bring the sons of Israel out of Egypt?" (Exodus 3:11) He became who he was by accepting his vocation in spite of his self-distrust.

The self-identity problem has become a major cause of anxiety in our time for several reasons. The most obvious one is that in our world of big cities, big organizations, and ever-changing technology, the individual has a hard time being himself or herself. At times all of us feel we are no more than tiny cogs in a gigantic machine. In the small towns and villages of an agricultural region, everybody knows everybody else. *That* has many drawbacks, of course, but not the drawback of being lost in a crowd of faces and counting for nothing—being a number instead of a name. Increasingly we are being drawn into larger units: from the country to the town, from the town to the city, from the city to the super–city. And with each move, it is less easy to know who we are and to be known for what we are.

The tragedy is that in the situation where it is difficult to be an individual, we are in danger of losing just those supports that might help us. In the family we get our first ideas of the different roles men and women can play in society. Yet the family gives all too little help. Even if it is not divided, depriving the children of seeing how a man and woman can cooperate to make a home, it is usually a place where there are just two adults. In previous times the family may have included grandparents, an unmarried uncle or aunt, and sometimes distant relatives who were being "given a home." In these days of city apartments and small suburban homes, this sort of multiple setup has ceased to exist. So a growing child knows few adults in an intimate way and is confined more and more to companions of his own age.

In his wise and witty book *An Offering of Uncles,* Robert Capon has written: *"Any ten-year-old boy who would not rather live with his Uncle Henry is a boy to be watched with the gravest suspicion."* [10] Robert Capon's point is that uncles (and aunts) are a child's most natural contacts with the adult world. Because a child's parents are special protection-and-authority figures, they cannot introduce the child as well to the way adults behave and to the matters that interest adults. Parents are involved too closely with their children to take them simply as budding human beings. Besides, a father or mother is only one person, and children need to see many examples of what adulthood means. Alas, if a child has uncles and aunts today, they are likely to be scattered across the nation and seldom are visited. Then, too, our way of living cuts down the possibility of neighbors being thrown together often enough that they become honorary aunts and uncles to the children nearby.

Someone has said that no artist ever began a career as a painter by saying to himself, "I want to paint." Seeing the work of some artist gave him the urge to paint and made him vow to himself, "I am going to paint pictures *like that.*" The same is true with identity. We become ourselves by first having a model to copy. Then, as we follow another person's footsteps, we get into our own particular stride and find a path of our own.

THE GENERATION GAP

The much-discussed generation gap, like the identity crisis, is a part of life in every age. And, like the identity crisis, it has become especially obvious and unusually painful in recent years.

God made mankind for community. But mankind has fallen, and all his relationships are out of order. Paul explains that fallen persons are those "who hold the truth in unrighteousness" (Romans 1:18, KJV). Paul's words put into modern language would sound something like this: fallen persons are those who get hold of an important idea, like the generation gap, but they get it all wrong.

Parents bring children into the world. They do not remain children but become persons in their own right. Because parents know they are responsible for their children, they are properly concerned that their children not undo their years of care and concern before they have learned to be fully responsible for themselves. Children know that they can learn responsibility only when they are trusted with it. They can be persons in their own right only when they have cut the apron strings. Yet who can tell when that time has come? The parents keep insisting *not yet,* and the children frantically demand *no longer.* Not always is it possible to say who is right. Certainly there will be times when neither will give way. As physical birth is painful, so birth of personhood is painful, and often long and drawn out. Sometimes it is fatal.

The generation gap cannot be closed completely. For the world in which parents have battled is not the same world into which their children go to play their part. On the other hand, the world is probably not as different as the children like to think. For this reason the gap that has widened during adolescence and adulthood can often be closed again if relationships have not been severely damaged. As Ecclesiastes said, there is a time for everything under heaven:

> a time to kill, and a time to heal;
> a time to break down, and a time
>   to build up.
>   (Ecclesiastes 3:3)

Said a young man nearing twenty, "I used to think Dad hadn't a clue about anything. But it is surprising what the old man has learned during the last year or two."

If the breakdown of the parent-child relationship has started with the breakdown of the marriage relationship, the generation gap becomes much wider than need be; and it turns into a kind of demon that seems to have a life of its own. When the child does not trust the adult world, and when he finds no adult models he wishes to copy, love turns into hate. At this point relationships depend upon the existence of a remnant of trust that can continue through the period of antagonism to bring later healing. Like opposing armies on a battlefield, the generations take their stand and the battle cry goes up, "Never trust anyone over thirty!"

Thirty, incidentally, is about the age when adult responsibilities have to be accepted. By that time, young people have to consider seriously whether they are to get married or to become reconciled to a single life. If they are already married, their children are no longer infants but are coming to the age when they have to be disciplined in preparation for adulthood. At thirty an individual cannot be trusted to be a single-minded warrior harrassing the Establishment. Already in varying ways he is being enlisted into the ranks of that Establishment which a rising generation will have to oppose.

The generation gap, which might be described as a sensitivity gap or an understanding gap, is a creation of fallen man and at odds with God's plan of creation. It is a glaring example of Paul's "truth in unrighteousness," for it divides the community of mankind into warring factions.

THE LONELY INDIVIDUAL

Mankind was created for relationship and only through relationships can the individual become a person. When the baby is in its mother's womb, it makes no decision about any relationship. The relationship of complete dependence upon the mother, however, ends with birth, and gradually a new individual evolves, a person in his own right. How he is related to others may be determined largely by his experience of how others relate to him in his formative years. Yet, because he is a person, the decision of relationships is his to make if he wills to make it.

Loneliness comes from rejecting or misusing relationships. Loneliness does not come from being physically alone. We never feel so lonely as when we are in a crowd that is hurrying by without seeming to care for us. Being isolated from others does not necessarily mean being lonely. Thoreau, living alone in Walden wood, felt at peace with himself and in living unity with all mankind.

Loneliness is the most terrifying of today's evils and one of the commonest. The title of a popular book describes modern society's predicament—*The Lonely Crowd*. We are all crowded together and terribly alone. The rising suicide rate and the increase in mental illness are indications that something is wrong with us.

The lonely individual is not fully a person. He is uncertain about his identity; that is why he is lonely. He looks about for someone else to complete his identity, to tell him who he is. He is starving for relationship, not knowing how to "relate."

Never have people tried so hard to have relationships; perhaps this indicates the extent of our fall from God's intention for us. Psychiatry has become the hope of thousands, and recent years have seen a boom in techniques of group therapy and "human relationship" courses. The latter bring people together physically in the hope that by being forced into contact with others they will be enabled to find satisfactory relationships with them. Yet the high claims made for all these techniques do not seem to answer the needs that are so evident. For, coinciding with the growth of these techniques is the rapid spread of astrology, witchcraft, belief in magic, and fortune-telling. People who cannot find personal relationships hope that impersonal forces—the stars, the Tarot pack, I-Ching divination, and the rest—will bring them a full life and a fulfilled selfhood.

All of these hopes have a common failing: they overlook the fact of creation that loneliness is not the result of being alone, but of lacking relationships that make a full human life. To be a person is to be able to be alone, physically, and to know how to live with that aloneness without being lonely. Just because we are able to enter into relationships does not mean that we shall always find the exact relationships we would like, when and where we want them. To be often lonely is part of living, yet it need not cause us to feel condemned to loneliness.

Finally, religious faith is the one thing that can banish loneliness. We can easily understand why the twenty-third psalm is the best-known passage in the Bible. This psalm speaks of the relationship that no isolation can remove: "The Lord is my shepherd; I shall not want." We can understand also why this psalm is used so often at the time of death when each individual is completely alone. For the finality of another person's death reminds us that no human companionship lasts forever.

To be afraid of being alone is to be afraid of life, for no life is without experiences of isolation. Furthermore, in our having to stand alone sometimes, there is the possibility of our becoming real persons with real relationships. But the decision is ours—alone. Luther said: "Every one must do his own believing, just as every one must do his own dying."

DENYING LONELINESS: ALCOHOL AND SEX

People try different ways of escaping loneliness. But the only true way of overcoming loneliness is to come to an understanding of what it means to be a person who must face the lonely state. Only in this way can an individual find the support of other persons. Those who are afraid to be alone can never know the support of other persons in a relationship of mutual trust.

The ways of escape that people try end in futility because they all begin by trying to deny the fact of human solitariness. And, in order to accomplish this, they make believe that human beings can live without facing their separate and independent responsibilities. Thus they deny the need for the individual to be a real person.

The alcoholic denies loneliness by drinking himself into a condition where he is no longer physically responsible for himself. Medical men point out that the genuine alcoholic is unable to stop drinking, once he begins, because the unconscious drive toward oblivion controls him completely. Having taken this way of denying his loneliness, he is no longer a person but a slave ruled by a master. Therefore, as organizations such as Alcoholics Anonymous have found out, the alcoholic desperately needs the support of other persons who can strengthen his will to be a person. He needs support to avoid taking a backward step along the path that will lead him to self-destruction.

Sex is another, though more subtle, means of denying the solitary state of the human being. In sexual union man and woman lose the sense of their separateness. For persons responsibly related to each other in a total life relationship, the sexual act becomes a final expression of their relatedness. But, when this personal relation is lacking, indulging in the sex act is simply a way of finding a temporary escape from one's individuality and the loneliness of being a single human being.

This search for an escape from loneliness is illustrated in John Updike's novel *Couples*. Though this book is often considered just a lurid account of a number of sexual adventures, it is written as a report on the fallen individual in present-day society. To begin with, the title *Couples* indicates its theme. The husbands and wives who begin, at first guiltily, to exchange partners are those who have lost all understanding of community in the biblical sense. They have no genuine regard for the children for whom they are responsible. They search for a life they can live as *couples,* finding in sex the sole purpose of living. Foxy Whitman, the female of the central couple in the book, reveals the motive behind their searching when she writes to her lover Piet Hanema: *"I remember lovemaking as an exploration of a sadness so deep people must go in pairs, one cannot go alone."* [11] In *Couples* Updike shows how such "exploration" may seem to be the business of those who try the experiments in sexual exchanges. But because this is not a world of couples but a world where man and woman are the basic units of the human community, human life itself is involved—all persons are responsible for other persons. The central action in the book is Foxy's abortion which Piet insists upon because he is not willing to admit his personal responsibility toward the next generation.

THE BODY OF DEATH

Some people attempt to deny loneliness by turning away from their lives as persons. The rapid growth of what is called the "drug culture" is one indication of this denial.

As with alcohol, people resort to drugs when they cannot face their existence as separate individuals who have a burden of loneliness. Unlike the alcoholic, though, the drug user is not always an addict. Drugs are sought out deliberately for their power to transport the user to a happiness that comes from the loss of a sense of self, time, and space. Some drugs popular today have been used for centuries in religious cults. No doubt the "drug culture" has gained a hold upon the young because they are in search of something more than what they find in the society of their elders. Cut off from their religious roots in Christianity, they find a religious substitute in the self-dissolving "esctasy" of the drugged state.

These "trips" are, however, as unsatisfactory and as self-defeating as are other avenues of escape from personhood. The dull world is always there when the drugged person returns to himself. Instead of being helped to fulfill himself, the drug user becomes less able to deal with the responsibilities of society. In addition, he finds that his particular choice of a way to overcome loneliness has dug one more ditch separating him from human relationships. Society now has the additional problem of dealing with drug users and preventing them from destroying others.

As personal life becomes more divided and as relationships are broken, dissatisfaction with the existing community continues to grow. Another path of escape from loneliness appears: the path of revolution. While some turn inward, either by using drugs or by adopting the teachings of a religious cult that denies the separate existence of the self, others turn outward and hope to smash society as it now functions. They believe that the overthrow of the Establishment will result in a new and free society where community will be possible.

Revolutionary beliefs, of course, exist in different patterns, some more realistic than others. Often they spring, not from deliberately chosen political policies, but from dread of loneliness in individuals. In the revolutionary community the individual can lose himself in the "movement." His responsibilities are chosen for him. By following the simple aims of the group to which he belongs, he is relieved of having to work out difficult choices. He has a place assigned to him. He has a place to *be*.

Paul spoke of the condition of the fallen person as being bound in by "a body of death." Death is indeed the end of all attempts to deny human solitariness and human responsibility for community.

TEACHING-LEARNING SUGGESTIONS

Topic Question

What are some of the causes and some of the effects of the present-day crisis of identity?

Goal

Decide if and why it is important for you to answer the topic question. You may want to reword the question or to write your own. Then decide what you want to find out in order to answer your question.

Preview of the Lesson

(This outline of the main ideas in the chapter and the related questions are to aid the leader who chooses the lecture-discussion method of teaching.)

1. In contemporary America, persons are seeking an answer to the question "Who am I?"
   a. Modern life makes self-definition difficult.
   b. The trend toward stereotyping and "pigeon-holing" persons denies individuals their uniqueness.
2. Identity formation ideally comes about in the family.
   a. Sexual identification is the first step in self-definition.
   b. Adults outside the family play a major role in helping a child understand his sexual role and his self-image.
3. Identity formation begins with an attempt to follow a model; later, the individual discovers his own uniqueness.
4. The generation gap is a gap in understanding, sensitivity, and empathy between generations.
   a. The generation gap can never be closed entirely without destroying the individuality of all persons involved.
   b. But the period marked by bitterness about the generation gap can be a time for growing, sharing, and a learning to respect the "otherness" of each person.
5. A lack of self-identity and the conflict of the generation gap bring about a deep sense of loneliness in many persons.
   a. Loneliness comes from rejecting or misusing relationships.
   b. Persons seek a way out of loneliness by a variety of life-denying means such as alcohol and drugs, "consciousness-expanding" experiences, and so on.
      (1) Loneliness is not a lack of relationships; it is a characteristic of the quality of relationships.
      (2) Religious faith, a right relationship with God, overcomes loneliness for it provides the individual with the only permanent and unchanging relationship.

Related Questions to Discuss

1. When have you felt the need to answer the question "Who am I?" What kinds of circumstances cause you to ask this

question? What do you do when you sense a need to answer this question?

2. What factors in our culture make it difficult for a man or a woman to know who he or she is?

3. When you were a child, who was your major model of adulthood? Why this person over others?

4. Is the generation gap unique in intensity in our time? If your answer is *yes*, how has our present culture created this gap?

5. "There is no way of closing the generation gap completely." How can persons learn to live with a generation gap?

6. How do you experience loneliness? In what situations do you feel lonely though surrounded by close friends? In what situations do you feel unlonely though no friends are near?

7. Do women experience loneliness differently from men? Are the causes of a woman's loneliness the same as the causes of a man's loneliness? Illustrate your answers.

8. In what ways do persons in your community strive to overcome loneliness? Do persons ever use the church as a place and activity to overcome loneliness? How?

9. How might the Christian church lead society to a sense of community that would overcome loneliness?

(The suggestions below are designed to aid leaders and groups desiring a variety of teaching-learning techniques. Choose and adapt those suggestions best suited to the needs of your group.)
Begin

As persons arrive for this session, supply them with paper and pencil and ask them to write completions for the following sentence stems:

The modern identity crisis is caused by ――――――.

What is really behind the generation gap is ――――――.

Persons experience loneliness because ――――――.

Let the group members retain their completed sentences for use at the conclusion of the session.

Continue

Have ready a supply of magazines, colored paper, crayons, scissors, tape, and rubber cement or paste. Let each person working individually construct a picture or collage that suggests to him a definition of himself. Some persons may want to cut pictures from magazines; others may choose to draw pictures or designs that illustrate their self-understanding. Or some may choose to write a short paragraph defining themselves. Let those who will share their creations with the whole group. What insights did you gain into your own self-identity from this experience?

As a whole group, share examples from motion pictures, books, or television programs of persons caught in loneliness. How did loneliness affect the persons in these illustrations? How was the loneliness resolved? Does our contemporary culture depict a true picture of loneliness and its causes? Give reasons for your answer.

Conclude

Look again at the statements you wrote individually as this session opened. How might you change your sentence endings as a result of your discussion in this session? Let several persons share their sentence endings with the whole group.

7
the way back to: community

LEO M. JOHNSON

Scripture: **Luke 15:2-32**
The parables of the lost sheep, the lost coin, and the lost son remind us of the need for active concern if what is lost is to be restored.

"For the Son of man is come to save that which was lost" (Matthew 18:11, KJV). Jesus came to restore broken relationships, beginning with the relationship of mankind to God. Christians must be concerned to bring the message of Jesus into all areas of contemporary life, and so into the lives of men and women in their relationships with each other.

The message of Jesus was first of all a message of repentance. Before he could repent man had to recognize where he had gone wrong in relation to God's will for him in creation. Only when the Prodigal Son had "come to himself" did he turn his steps toward his father's home. We are called to examine our way of living to see where it is contradicting God's intention for mankind. When we realize that we are on the wrong road there is a chance for us to find the right road—the road to the Father's love for us that leads to the love of our neighbor.

Recently we have heard much talk about "celebrating" life. Life in harmony with God is indeed worth celebrating, for it is the *abundant life* promised by Jesus (John 10:10). But the unredeemed life is not to be celebrated but to be repented of. Similarly much is being said about Christian faith being the faith that makes us free. But freedom brings happiness only if it is the freedom of the "sons of God" (Romans 8:14). Otherwise, both celebration and freedom will bear bitter fruits. After the night of celebrating, the drunkard rises in the morning to meet a hangover, unpaid bills, and the reproaches of his family. After rejoicing in his freedom from the restraints of home, the Prodigal found himself a stranger in a foreign land. If there is no repentance and no turning back toward home, the end is cynicism and despair.

NO EASY RETURN TO EDEN

In Chapter 3 we spoke about the male American dream of a New World in which men could live free from the evils of the Old World civilization. Today the New World has ceased to be a wilderness and has become the most highly urbanized and industrialized country upon earth. America is both the heir of Western European civilization and frequently its defender and upholder. In this situation, the old American dream still lingers on, but it is increasingly hard to believe in. Away from our television screens, where Westerns continue to be among the most popular programs, the manly Adam facing an untamed and womanless world is less than real.

Still we yearn to return to an Eden of innocence and unguilty happiness. In John Updike's novel *Couples* this theme is illustrated. We said in the last chapter that *Couples* presents a picture of fallen humanity. The story shows a portion of society living by its own prescription for happiness and ignoring God's intention for mankind. Updike makes clear that the people in his novel imagine that they have found a way to escape the consequences of the Fall and that they live as though they were in Eden.

Updike's couples think that they can re-enter Eden because the consequences of the Fall—painful work and child-bearing—seem to be removed from their lives. The men are, on the whole, comfortably well off, and the women's fears of unwanted pregnancies have been removed by the Pill. Still, they are fallen persons, although they try to close their eyes to the fact. They start with an ideal of "an essential fidelity [faithfulness in marriage] set in a matrix of easy and open companionship among couples." [12] But this ideal crumbles into a series of sordid adulteries and evasions, jealousies and open hatreds. When the pretense of fidelity finally breaks down and two husbands openly exchange wives, one of the wives is briefly conscience-stricken. She says to her partner, "Now we're really corrupt. All of us." But he simply replies, "Do you think it matters on the moon?" [13]

The characters in *Couples* fail to understand their plunge into total corruption because they are unaware that mankind is already corrupt and ripe for further corruption except for the grace of God restraining them. However, since they have no faith in God, they will acknowledge no restraint. For them the heavens are empty; what significance does anything that happens on earth have beyond the place and moment of its happening? The cold and lifeless moon is indifferent to life on earth, and to them, the moon is all there is beyond this earth. Since life has no final meaning, the enjoyment of the moment is all that matters.

On the dust jacket of *Couples* is William Blake's picture of Adam and Eve asleep in Eden before the Fall. The noble and serene forms of man's first parents as drawn by Blake make an ironic contrast to the petty, backbiting behavior of the couples described in the book. Of course, none of Updike's couples consciously compare themselves with Adam and Eve. For them the story of the Fall is an old legend unrelated to modern life. But Updike makes us see that life today has all the features of the biblical message about man's created state.

In reality, the unconscious desire to find Eden lies behind the way most people today think about marriage. The cult of the Girl could not be so widespread and attractive if man did not think of himself as an unfallen Adam seeking to be united with his Eve. Through divorce and remarriage the search to find the ideal Eve is continued, in spite of failure. For each failure of this dream does not weaken its appeal: the *next* time perhaps the perfect Girl will appear; the *next* love will prove to be the true and lasting love.

Experience does not seem to teach that there is no easy return to Eden. The Fall, as Christian faith teaches, is reversed only through faith in God's appointed Savior, Jesus Christ. And faith in Jesus must begin with repentance, with the understanding of our fallen state, and with the prayer for the grace of God that alone can restore us.

FAITH AND FIDELITY

Couples shows that fallen man has some idea of fidelity but does not have in him the power to make it live. *Faith* and *fidelity* are basically the same words, from the Latin word *fides* meaning trust. Without faith it is impossible to please God (Hebrews 11:6). And without faithfulness or fidelity it is impossible to love our neighbors. For faith is an openness to relationship. We are opened by faith to the loving will of God. And fidelity means keeping faith, continuing in the relationship we have opened ourselves to. Repentance leads to faith and faith makes reconciliation possible, in effect, reversing the Fall. By faith continued in fidelity we can find the way back to community.

Fidelity has a very special place in the relationship between man and woman, as well as being basic to every part of human community. We cannot live together without trust and without loyalty. People are prepared to make sacrifices for the common good, to uphold the rules of their labor unions or their professions, and to defend their country. But, because the basic unit of society is the family, fidelity between man and woman comes before all other concerns.

Most people do not think of the man-woman relationship in that way. They consider their partnership something for them to decide upon—a personal matter for two people to work out between themselves. If a soldier deserts the Army, it is a very serious matter. Without the loyalty of its citizens, a country will soon cease to exist. If either labor or management refuses to honor contracts, the whole economy will be thrown into chaos. But a broken home does not show the same sort of immediate large-scale effect. Children of a broken home are provided for and will grow up somehow. They may even gain by a legal separation through not having to live in a house where there is constant quarreling. Life does go on, and society is not torn apart or made impossible when a man and a woman break their marriage vows and decide to put an end to an unsatisfactory relationship.

Yes, the man-woman relationship *is* a personal thing. And this is why the laws of society have to recognize that not all marriages are going to last. But the relationship is personal in the deepest and most serious sense; it involves people—not just one pair of persons but, directly or indirectly, everyone with whom that one pair have relationships. And it involves more than one generation of persons. Although the relationship has no obvious effect upon society at large, ultimately it influences the whole character of society, determining social health and social integrity.

The tremendous importance of the man-woman relationship is not that it concerns couples. Actually, it never concerns *a* couple, a single pair of human beings, except perhaps in the intimacy of the sex act. Even there a third person must be considered—the child who is or is not conceived during the act. Further, we must not discount the influence this act will have upon encouraging or discouraging fidelity between man and woman in their society.

When a man and a woman meet, they are always Adam and Eve. Certainly, they are fallen Adam and fallen Eve belonging to a fallen society. Though Adam and Eve fell they were still the parents of all living. Each modern Adam and Eve are the parents of the future generations of mankind. They have chosen their part, and they must acknowledge their responsibilities. If they reject fidelity to each other, they have chosen to be unfaithful to all who come after them.

THE SHARED LIFE

Fidelity between man and woman means a shared life, one that offers the possibility of true community. Marriage holds a promise of community, because mankind is present in the two different kinds created by God. By being faithful to their promise to live together for each other and the human community, man and woman are remembering God's intention for the human race.

The shared life of marriage must be permanent if man and wife are to become "one flesh." They enjoy a unique relationship in knowing each other through their sexual differences. For the husband, his wife is "the woman." For the wife, her husband is "the man." Together they form a wholeness of humanity unknown anywhere else. Through their intimacy, they catch a fleeting and imperfect glimpse of what life could be like when lived entirely within the intention of God. In a sense, they discover a partial return to Eden. At the same time, they cannot wipe out the consequences of the Fall. Though understand their shared life as God's intention for male and female, they never succeed in being completely "one flesh." And because they cannot share life perfectly, they still experience loneliness. This is true not only when their trust in each other breaks down momentarily or when they are reminded of the guilt of fallen existence, but also when they remember that they live in a fallen society. Their ways of thinking about each other and of treating each other are influenced by the fallen society in which they have been reared. So, distortion of human relationships is present even when the man and the woman are most happy in each other's company and rejoicing in their shared life.

How much social custom shapes our thinking about the differences between man and woman! The beauty and the sustaining power of married life flow from the differences between male and female. The physical differences that determine intercourse and reproduction are constant; but, beyond that, maleness and femaleness have no unaltering and unalterable characteristics. This is clearly evident in the different forms family life takes in different ages and in different countries. And probably maleness and femaleness mean slightly different things for every marriage. After all, we are persons, not robots turned out on a production line.

The shared life, then, cannot be exactly the same for any two pairs of married partners. Discovery of what this life can be is one of the rewarding wonders of the married state. A lifetime is needed for a man and a woman to discover just how they complement each other, the strengths of the one compensating for the weaknesses in the other. Thus no marriage is completely predictable in its happiness or in its times of strain and bitterness. Each marriage is unique—as the two who become "one flesh" are a unique example of fulfilled humanity.

Preconceived ideas of what a man or a woman should be are disastrous in their effect upon marriage simply because they do not take into account the uniqueness of any marriage. The role of the male in sexual intercourse is relatively a dominating one and the role of the female a relatively submissive one. A man is said to "take" a woman, a woman to "give herself" to a man. But to generalize this one aspect of male-female partnership as the pattern for the whole marriage relationship is to forget that the partners are persons and not abstract types of maleness and femaleness.

Even in the realm of sexual experience, all such generalizations are misleading. Accepting them has led in the past to the distorted view that the male alone is active in sexual relations, while the female is passive. This view is less common today because of the wide circulation of physiological information on sexual matters. But it still colors much thinking about man-woman relations. Many people, both men and women, imagine that a man is not a red-blooded male if he does not adopt an aggressive, dominating attitude to women in particular and to the world in general. Regarding females, a woman is thought to be less than a woman if she does not obviously dress and act in a way that will attract male attention.

To be truly personal, the shared life cannot follow any popular social stereotypes. Its reality lies in its infinite variety. Beyond the constant of sexual intercourse, there are innumerable ways of becoming "one flesh"—as many ways as there are partners. The shared life should be full of variety and surprise.

MORE THAN COUPLES

We have said that thinking of married partners only as couples gives a totally wrong view of the married state. A married pair is never simply a couple, since these two form the basic foundation for a complete human community. Each sexual act can become the link between the generations.

The man-woman relationship shared in marriage opens the partners to involvement with other people who are known primarily as *persons*. If they have children they also have responsibility for persons whose maleness or femaleness becomes a direct concern. Each partner has a distinct role here, while together they give each child an image of what the partnership between male and female can mean. But, while it is always true that mankind comes in two different sorts, it is also true that parents must be concerned first of all with their children as persons. By the time children become deeply concerned about their roles as men and women, they must be able to take responsibility for their own maleness and femaleness. Parents cause disaster when they try to make decisions for their children after they have taken partners for themselves. The biblical command here is plain: "Therefore a man leaves his father and his mother and cleaves to his wife, and they shall become one flesh" (Genesis 2:24). We should notice that it is the *unfallen* Adam who makes this statement, immediately after Eve has been created. Fallen Adams and Eves are not always ready to accept this direction. Married children must "leave" father and mother in all matters that relate to their partnership, even if they happen to live under one roof with their parents.

Human community means distinct persons living their own lives, separately yet not in separation. The "leaving" of father and mother is the prelude to the coming into existence of new partnerships. Husband and wife are always more than a couple. If they have children, they are more than a couple with children. They are partners in human existence, having responsibility for helping other human beings of a different generation become part of the community of mankind.

One of the hardest things for parents to learn, and one of the most important, is that the children who seem to belong to them are not theirs at all. Children are persons-in-the-making, headed for a life of their own. Life styles change, and the decisions of grown children may be puzzling and even distressing to parents. The best that parents can do is to keep their own integrity as persons and show that they expect this from their children.

Yes, married partners are more than a couple. Their fidelity to each other is so important, not simply for their own experience of being "one flesh" but, beyond that, for introducing the next generation to the basic community that can be achieved through fidelity between man and woman.

THE COMMUNITY OF PERSONS

One of the most crucial problems of present-day society is the loss of the feeling of personal worth. Gigantic organizations make up the everyday world and cause the individual to feel lost and unwanted. Physically, we are dwarfed by the huge factories, office buildings, and apartment blocks that dominate our cities. If we happen to live in a house to ourselves this gain is offset by the fact that, in all likelihood, it is one of many similar houses on streets stretching for miles in the great urban sprawl. If we still live in a small town or the country, we have a feeling that life is passing us by; we belong to a style of life that is doomed to die, as the traffic streams by on the turnpikes and the superjets pass overhead. What is the individual today, except a number in whirling computers?

Nowhere do we feel more certain of being persons in our own right then we do in the home. There we are known in a way that cannot be recorded in a file or stored on computer cards. In the family we are remembered for what we were as well as for what we are. There are memories of us locked in contacts with those whom we have loved and who have loved us. In the family we were the focus of hopes and plans even before we were born.

So it is in the family that we know what human community, the community of persons, really is. When divisions and self-centered isolation of individual lives exist in the family, our only chance of knowing what community might be is lost or made very difficult. Couples may seek to escape individual loneliness by coming together in the desperate effort to feel needed by someone. Individuals can meet sexually, pass time together at work or in leisure hours, and take pleasure in each other's company. But they can do all this *without* becoming persons to each other. Becoming persons requires personal commitment and personal sacrifice.

Individuals need fidelity to blossom as persons. Unless the marriage promise of "for better, for worse" is taken with the utmost seriousness, couples are simply taking advantage of each other. When the benefits seem to wear thin, then all individuals will go their separate ways without caring what happens to the other except in a superficial and sentimental way. But, in the cementing of faithful partnership between a man and a woman, the way back to community is born. In the life of sharing that flows from this partnership persons are brought into the community. This community includes generations within its borders and opens up to give strength and hope to every individual that comes within its reach by making them feel certain of being persons. Ultimately, that community embraces all mankind. It is the promise of the restored community of the people of God.

TEACHING-LEARNING SUGGESTIONS

Topic Question
What steps are necessary for a man and a woman to discover the wholeness of humanity that God intended in creation?

Goal
Decide if and why it is important for you to answer the topic question. You may want to reword the question or to write your own. Then, decide what you want to find out in order to answer your question.

Preview of the Lesson
(This outline of the main ideas in the chapter and the related questions are to aid the leader who chooses the lecture-discussion method of teaching.)

1. Community has been broken by man's rejection of his relationship with God.
   a. Many persons attempt to live as if the Fall had never taken place.
   b. The way to community commences with repentance.
   c. The Fall is reversed only through faith in Christ Jesus.
2. Faith and fidelity are both built on trust and loyalty.
   a. Community cannot exist without trust and loyalty.
   b. For community to exist in society, trust and loyalty must be demonstrated between man and woman in the family as the basic relationship in any society.
3. The man-woman relationship has both a personal and a social dimension.
   a. Personally, it involves the commitment of two persons.
   b. Socially, the decisions made by those persons in that relationship can affect the character of society.
   c. Ultimately, a breakdown in the man-woman relationship leads to a breakdown of the whole social fabric.
4. Man and woman in shared community fulfill the intention of God.
5. The marriage relationship is built on differences, and each marriage is different from every other marriage.
6. Only in community can the individual discover his sense of personal worth and personal identity.
   a. The family is the source of the individual's understanding of community and of his own self-worth.
   b. The family may not realize God's intention of the shared life of community, but it holds the potential for helping persons discover community most directly.

Related Questions to Discuss
1. In what ways does our Christian faith make us free? Deal with this question by considering these questions: Free for what? Free to do what? Free from what?

2. How can a person know if his repentance is accepted? If he is forgiven? If his relationship with God is restored?
3. Is *Eden* a state of mind you have experienced? Or look forward to experiencing? Explain your answer.
4. Can a fallen Adam—a contemporary man—ever find the ideal Eve—the perfect Girl who will make his life a paradise? Why? Illustrate your answer with examples.
5. What adjustments are necessary in the marriage relationship when partners discover that the wife is not the ideal Girl or the husband the perfect Adam?
6. In what ways is the whole fabric of society affected by each broken relationship between a husband and wife?
7. How is faith lived out in a marriage? How is fidelity lived out in a marriage?
8. "The shared life . . . cannot follow any popular social stereotypes." How, then, can and do husband and wife discover their own life style and their own pattern for the shared life?
9. How do persons experience a sense of loss of worth?
10. Can persons sense their personal worth outside the marriage relationship? Illustrate your answer.
11. How can you know if your family is a community of faith and fidelity? What steps might you take to make it such a community if you sense that it is not?

(**The suggestions below are designed to aid leaders and groups desiring a variety of teaching-learning techniques. Choose and adapt those suggestions best suited to the needs of your group.**)
Begin

How does modern advertising coax a man into thinking he can live free, without responsibilities? As a whole group, cite examples. You would probably want to include commercials that suggest "getting away from it all" or advertisements that counsel "Live it up; you only go around once in life!" In what ways do such advertisements suggest that a man can discover Eden through "things"? Or through power over others? Or through status? What is missing from all such commercials? Why are such advertisements incomplete answers to a person's search for Eden?

Continue

Divide into two groups, the men in one group, the women in another. Let each group deal with questions such as these: What does it mean for a man and a woman to live in trust and loyalty? How is "faith continued in fidelity" lived out in the marriage relationship? Make your answers to these questions as practical as possible. Now let the two groups share the results of their discussions. Do men and women answer these questions similarly? If not, why not? Must men and women understand faith and fidelity exactly alike? Why?

THE WAY BACK TO COMMUNITY

"Human community means distinct persons living their own lives, separately yet not in separation" (page 101). Individually reflect on this sentence, then write a single sentence that explains for you the meaning of this statement. Collect the unsigned sentences and read some aloud. Do all agree on an understanding of the authors' meaning?

Conclude

Read John 15:1-8. What do these words of Christ say to your understanding of the wholeness of human community under the lordship of Christ?

8
the
dimension
of
the
body

RICK SMOLAN

Scripture: 1 Corinthians 7:1-21
           Paul advises Christians concerning marriage as the expression of the Christian life, renewed in the Spirit.

Persons—male and female—always have bodies, and these bodies are part of God's will for them. The prayer for Christians in the New Testament is:

> May the God of peace himself sanctify you wholly; and may your spirit and soul and body be kept sound and blameless at the coming of our Lord Jesus Christ.
> (1 Thessalonians 5:23)

The body has a place in God's plan for a redeemed humanity. And this means that sexuality has a place too, for it is the foundation for the difference between the two sorts of humanity decreed by God to be made for each other. Sexuality does not determine our lives as persons capable of living in community—being human does that. Yet sexuality is an essential part of our personal lives. If we fail to take account of it, we are forgetting the kind of creation we are. We are as God made us, and that includes our sexuality.

THE INTIMACY OF THE BODY

Our bodies are the most obvious evidence we have of who we are. They make us recognizable. The childhood names given us by our friends, such as "Shorty" or "Red," refer to some prominent physical feature that sets us apart from others. Our bodies also play a large part in making us what we are. If we are noticeably undersized, for example, that fact is likely to influence our personality. Some of the world's most aggressive personalities—Julius Caesar, Napoleon, Al Capone, Hitler, and Mussolini—were either unusually short or constitutionally weak. Physically, they felt compelled to make an extra effort to assert themselves and to "measure up" to their fellows. The opposite is also true: a great number of the "outstanding" men of history have been above average in size. They found it easy to imagine that they could excel among their fellows. (The leadership in industry, public life, and the churches contains a high proportion of outsized persons.)

Our bodies, though, are not what make us persons. Many efforts have been made to identify types of bodily physique and tie them to types of personality. The efforts have failed for lack of solid evidence. For a long time, people have tried to find out whether murderers have any common facial features that might help in identifying the kind of individual likely to become a killer. Alas, all of the photographs examined show that murderers have the same variety of features everybody else has. Asked to pick a possible criminal from a row of pictures, the chooser is quite likely to pick out a saintly clergyman or a conscientious social worker. Fat persons are said to be happy. Doctors are inclined to doubt this common opinion, and some definitely claim that fat persons are less happy than thin persons. The doctors go on to say that people are unhappy because they *make themselves* fat. The mind, not body, decides for all the extra pounds. However, medical opinion admits that we do not know why some people are inclined to stoutness and some not. What we do know is that there is an intimate connection between our bodies and the kind of person we are. But the body is not the controlling factor in deciding whether we are sad or happy persons, successes or failures, saints or sinners.

The same may be said about the question of whether our bodies are basically male or female. No absolute difference is apparent so far as male and female personalities are concerned. What we think to be manly or womanly results as much from what our society has come to expect men and women to be as from anything else. The few individuals who have had their sex changed medically because they are physiologically abnormal generally adjust to the new man or woman role, which they have chosen. Their problem lies in getting other persons to accept them in their altered role.

THE ROLE OF THE BODY

Our bodies, then, help to identify who we are. They are partly given us and partly the result of our choices in our way of living. The athlete and the office-worker with a heart condition think of themselves differently because everything they do is determined by the different capacities of their bodies. Yet, the office-worker might have been an athlete had he trained himself. And the athlete may develop a heart condition and be reduced to the same level of life style as the office-worker. What a person becomes is not directly dependent upon the kind of body he has, although his body is plainly an important part of his total make-up.

Chiefly, it seems, our body is important because it has such crucial bearing upon the way we encounter life and upon the range of our interests.

Some years ago members of a radio panel were asked to discuss the gifts they would give to a child at birth if they could play the part of the Good Fairy. One by one they said they would give the gift of good health. But one member of the panel, the British orchestral conductor Sir Malcolm Sargeant, disagreed. He had a daughter who had spent most of her childhood and early maturity in various tuberculosis sanitariums. Sir Malcolm said that prolonged illness, though a terrible deprivation, could waken and train a sensitivity lacking in those who had known only carefree healthiness. However, we cannot lightly deny that illness can also destroy personality. Jesus made healing one of the chief concerns of his ministry, calling attention to the relation of disease and sin. Yet, on the basis of their pastoral experience, every minister would agree that disease of the body is not the worst of evils, and that triumph *in* ill health can be even more impressive than triumph *over* ill health. St. Paul learned to accept his "thorn in the flesh" (certainly some form of physical affliction) as a challenge to show strength in weakness for the service of his Lord, even though he recognized the "thorn" as a "messenger of Satan" (2 Corinthians 12:7).

The role of the body, therefore, is a servant role; the body serves the whole personality. Our body has a large say in how our life is spent and what our aims and achievements shall be. But it cannot dictate the substance of our personal living, only its style. Like a servant it can give us freedom and ease, or it can rebel and bring pain. Our body cannot command us to be what we are not, and it cannot give us what we have not trained ourselves to want.

MAN'S BODY AND WOMAN'S BODY

The servant role of the body is true whether we happen to pass our lives as men or as women. Our bodies are at the same time a limitation and an opportunity, a binding and a freeing.

The most obvious difference between the physical lives of males and females lies in their reproductive systems. These differences make the life of a female more restricted than the life of a male. Women alone bear and suckle children, and both these activities may limit what women can do over a large part of their lives. Menstruation is an additional restriction—smaller but universal and long-continuing. Of course, not all women become mothers, and in highly developed countries only a portion of mothers breast-feed their children. So the most common restrictions upon a woman's freedom (bearing and nursing children) can be overcome to a very large extent, and perhaps entirely, through birth control and bottle-feeding. In this direction, the aims of Women's Liberation can be justified. A female working in society can meet her male counterpart on equal terms. Her woman's body need make little difference in her contribution to the world—provided male prejudice can be outgrown.

However, some physical differences of a more subtle kind cannot be put aside so easily. In reality, these differences may be much more important and much less easily ignored. Men and women do not grow to maturity at the same rate. Further, women's "weak" bodies are actually tougher than men's, and women have a longer life-expectancy

Lionel Tiger, an anthropologist (a student of the physical and mental characteristics of mankind, his social relationships, his customs, and so on) and author of *Men in Groups,* argues that the physical differences between men and women are in fact basic to the whole working of human society. Tiger, whose views are highly controversial, says that throughout human history there has been a division between the work done by women and the work done by men. This division is seen even in the animal kingdom and is particularly striking among the higher apes. Tiger believes that this division has its basis in the effect of sex hormones upon human behavior. The qualities of aggressiveness and self-assertion come from the sex hormone, testosterone; and the male has a vastly greater supply of this hormone. Thus the formation of social and political and military organizations that have made civilization possible has been the work of men. Men have become the formers of civilization, not because they have "suppressed" women's initiative in society, but because they have the physical drive that encourages them to attempt what women do not naturally wish to do. On the other hand, women have been concerned with rearing and caring for children, not because the task has been forced upon them, but because it goes along with their womanly capacities. Tiger's theory, needless to say, angers many women.

If the body is a servant and not a master, it should not dictate what people shall and must always do. Because a pattern of human life has existed for thousands or millions of years does not mean it must go unchanged until the end of time. Built-in differences between men's and women's bodies do not bind us like the laws of the Medes and the Persians "which alter not."

Nevertheless, our bodies are not servants that can be ordered about just as we please. We do not hire them or establish the terms of their service; it is the other way round. We can live healthily and normally only by keeping the rules that our bodies lay down. We do not make the rules for physical life, and we break them at our peril. If we choose to walk over a cliff, our bodies will plunge us to death. In the same way, the more subtle rules of physical life cannot be broken without self-destruction, though the consequences may not be so obvious.

If our bodies are to be the servants of our larger human purpose, we need more knowledge of their workings. Specialists in the study of the human body can provide us information and anthropologists can tell us how laws have worked in human societies so that we can work with them instead of against them. For example, Lionel Tiger believes that women's less aggressive nature may help us toward a more sane and peaceful society in the future. The more we know about the less obvious differences between male and female bodies, the better we can live as men and women sharing the task of restoring community for mankind.

SEXUALITY IS MORE THAN SEX

No longer do we think of the sex act as the central problem rising out of the physical difference between men and women. Interestingly, the scientific approach to the problem is remarkably close to the biblical and Christian view in making clear that sex, in the narrow sense of the word, is not central to human sexuality. Rather, at the center is the whole human community. And here the crucial question has to do with the relation between the generations.

Society must put the well-being of the young as its top priority so that the human race may live on. The differences between male and female go beyond the mechanisms for bringing about birth and sustaining physical life in early infancy. They are present in giving to each generation the means of growing up within a community of care. Physical human nature plays its part not only in giving birth and the milk necessary during the first months of life, but also in providing the basis for those psychological attitudes necessary for the offspring to grow to maturity and become parents of a new generation. The sexual differences that bring male and female together in order to have children also prepare the way for the specialized work that makes community possible. The physical conditions of motherhood prepare the mother for the task of teaching the child to become independent and, in due time, take up the role of being a man or a woman.

THE BODY IN HUMAN COMMUNITY

In a perfect society we can imagine that each individual would have the fullest enjoyment of all aspects of the human birthright. Each man and woman would have a sexual partner, each human couple would have children, each home would be a little community of love within the care of a greater community that would reach out to embrace all mankind. In such a state of well-being, our bodies would enjoy every natural satisfaction in a perfect sharing of all natural good.

But our society is a society of fallen human nature. St. Augustine of Hippo, the great Christian bishop of the fifth century, said, "Sin is the punishment of sin." We can see how true his words are when we look around us. Today's problems that are so difficult to solve are the bitter legacy of our past sins and the sins of our ancestors. For example, the evil of slavery leaves as its punishment the rage of the black man over white supremacy. The end of slavery did not bring about reconciliation between white and black, for sin does not cancel itself out. And the problem of the races would remain even if all remnants of white racism were to be destroyed—which is far from being a fact. The same is true of our sins against the sexuality of mankind.

As we have argued, perhaps our greatest sin in the area of sexuality is our lack of understanding that sexuality should serve the human community. Far too often we have thought of sexuality simply as sex to be used in the service of individual selfishness. If human community is to be restored along the lines of God's intention at creation, we shall have to repent of our actions that have frustrated true community throughout history. In recent years, Women's Liberation has reminded us that the pattern of male dominance with its sexual inequalities is still almost as strong as is racial bigotry. Even the goal of sexual equality is not enough in itself. In actual practice, the ideal of equality can take us only so far along the road to true community, and it can even produce conflict and hostility rather than partnership between the sexes, which is its aim. Justice within the law may require strict equality where women are presently discriminated against. Her sex should not exclude a woman from the vocation of her choice. But neither should the abstract idea of equality keep us from recognizing that in some types of work women surpass men, and in other types men are more suited than women. The wrong is done when mere prejudice excludes a woman from doing tasks she knows herself to be capable of doing.

One obvious injustice in society is its attitude toward single women. (Single men are viewed differently by society.) The single woman who does not find a partner but continues to work to support herself is almost invariably an object of pity or scorn. She is judged both by men and by other women as a sexual failure. This is particularly true if she is passed by in the marriage market because she is considered sexually unattractive. Even if she deliberately turns away from marriage, preferring personal freedom or devotion to work, the judgment is the same. The so-called "career" woman is considered unfeminine. She is thought to be an oddity, most likely bossy and unsympathetic, particularly to younger women still in the marriage market. Because people often live up to the popular image of themselves, the single woman may become that kind of person.

Legal equality alone will not solve the problem of the single woman, any more than anti-discrimination laws alone will solve the race problem. So long as the popular image of the career woman persists, it will arouse feelings of hostility toward her. If, through personal force of character and integrity, she gains acceptance, she will still be considered a strange exception to a universal rule. Our whole attitude toward the unmarried person needs to change.

The change can come about by understanding that sexual union is only a small part of sexuality. Change cannot be made effective simply by extending our present dominant ideas about sex to include women equally. For example, agreeing that the single woman should have freedom for extra marital sex, a freedom *assumed* to exist for men, is not a satisfactory way of understanding sexuality. Quite apart from the moral issue involved, women do not react to casual sexual encounters in the same way as men. (Of course, this does not mean that casual sex is any more "natural" for men than it is for women or any more "depraved" for women than it is for men.) The problem of the single woman can be solved only when a woman's femininity is not judged by whether she is sexually desired or has had sexual experience.

Celibacy, the taking of a vow of singleness, is another matter requiring greater understanding in society. Celibacy is not for everyone, either male or female. As Jesus himself taught, it is a calling to special individuals (Matthew 19:12). Choosing the celibate life should not set an individual off from the rest of humanity, marking that person as unnatural or, at any rate, distinctly odd.

Celibacy has a poor image today. One sign of this is the great unrest among Catholic priests resulting from the changes set into motion by Vatican II. Part of this unrest is a sane, understandable anticipation of genuine reform within the church organization. The rule requiring celibacy for all priests is an example of medieval legalism that may have had real purpose under social conditions of the past but does not make sense to the present Western World. Yet the harshness of the rule hardly explains the reaction against it. An estimated two hundred priests in North America leave the priesthood each year, almost all of them to marry. Probably the contemporary notion that a celibate cannot be a normal member of society has much to do with it. Both priests and their people regard celibacy as a barrier that prevents them from standing close to one another and understanding one another.

The wisdom of this notion is hardly self-evident, although its strength and widespread acceptance are clear enough. If celibacy is thought to be something unattractive and strange, and if the celibate person is considered to be someone who is lacking in full humanity, is the fullness of humanity really understood and appreciated? Or is the human person made less valuable and given less dignity if his maleness or femaleness is thought to be tied to being one of a couple? Can freedom to marry, made into the rule that only the married are fully human, actually take away the freedom to be a true person? Does the celibate person, who sacrifices the joy of the body and the joy of family life for the sake of serving the family of mankind, by that decision become alienated from mankind?

Unfortunately, these questions are too seldom raised in today's world. Yet they surely deserve deep and serious pondering. For the attitudes that underlie them are related to society's understanding of the sexuality of all persons, not just the unmarried.

TEACHING-LEARNING SUGGESTIONS

Topic Question
What part does the physical body play in the personality and character of the man and the woman?

Goal
Decide if and why it is important for you to answer the topic question. You may want to reword the question or to write your own. Then, decide what you want to find out in order to answer your question.

Preview of the Lesson
(This outline of the main ideas in the chapter and the related questions are to aid the leader who chooses the lecture-discussion method of teaching.)

1. Our bodies are as much a dimension of our personhood as our minds and our spirits.
   a. Our bodies are part of God's creation; they are good.
   b. Our bodies are the most obvious evidence of our personhood for they identify us to others.
2. Our bodies help determine our self-image.
   a. Our perception of our bodies has an effect on the way we see ourselves.
   b. The way we see ourselves affects directly the way we relate to others and to the world.
3. The body may affect the *life style* of a person, but the body is not the determiner of the character of that person.
   a. The body can both free or limit an individual.
   b. But the body must always be seen in a "servant role," not in the role of the ultimate dictator of the personhood of an individual.
4. Male and female bodies are different, providing different limitations and opportunities for men and women.
   a. Child-bearing and menstruation are physical limitations, but child-bearing is also a unique opportunity.
   b. The female body matures earlier, lives longer, and in some ways may be more durable than the male body.
5. Both men and women are limited by the fragility and mortality of the physical body; these can be accepted limitations or life-stifling concerns and preoccupations.
6. Physical sexuality—more than intercourse—provides for reproduction, the nurturing of young, and the division of labor that makes community possible.
7. Human sexuality must serve God's intention for human community, not individual selfishness.

Related Questions to Discuss
1. In what ways does our contemporary culture teach persons to reject or to be ashamed of their bodies? Cite examples.

2. What is the difference between *proper care* of the body as a gift of God and an *overconcern* with the body that makes the body not a servant but the master of the person?

3. In what ways has your body affected the way you encounter life? Think here of your bodily limitations and physical restrictions. Can you share your feelings about your body?

4. What is the difference between a person's *style* of personal living and that person's character of life? Give examples. How does the body affect each?

5. In what ways do persons become aware of their bodies? In what ways can parents help children develop a healthy physical self-image?

6. What is the role of bodily attractiveness in the relationship between a man and a woman?

7. In what ways is a female more physically restricted than a man? In what ways is a man more physically restricted than a woman? What, if anything, might you conclude about the relationship between men and women based on relative physical restrictions?

8. How does sexuality serve God's intention for human community?

9. In what ways can the single person be a part of and contribute to human community? What changes must society make in order to help the single person sense his full acceptance by others?

(The suggestions below are designed to aid leaders and groups desiring a variety of teaching-learning techniques. Choose and adapt those suggestions best suited to the needs of your group.)
Begin

Commence this session by considering the ways the body determines life style. Use some of these questions as discussion starters: What changes did you wish you could make in your body as a child? What changes do you wish you could make now? Why would you want to make these changes? How would your life style be different if your body type were different? If your body had been different throughout your life, how might your personality and your character have been affected?

Continue

"Our bodies are at once a limitation and an opportunity, a binding and a freeing." In groups of four, cite examples or illustrations to support or refute this statement. Then, as a whole group, list specific ways physical limitations and restrictions can be minimized, and opportunities recognized.

Hear a panel consisting of an elementary school teacher, a church school teacher, a parent, and a doctor or nurse discuss the ways in which children develop a physical self-image. The panel might focus also on ways the home and family can help persons develop a positive bodily self-image. If a panel discussion cannot be arranged, share your own experiences of developing a physical self-image. Can you develop a set of guidelines for helping children gain a healthy perspective on their bodies?

Refer to Chapter 1 in this book on the Sexual Revolution. How do some aspects of the Sexual Revolution deny God's will for sexuality as a means to community? What aspects further God's will in this direction? Be as specific as possible in your answer.

Conclude

Consider the status of single persons within your church. Is singleness recognized in your church and community as a legitimate option to marriage? Support your answer with reasons. How might your minister relate more effectively to those who have remained single?

LEO M. JOHNSON

9
the dimension of the mind

Scripture: Philippians 2:1-18
Paul commends the mind or human consciousness of Jesus as the pattern for Christian living.

"Just like a woman!" is the frequent comment of many a young husband faced by some puzzling statement or action on the part of his wife. Mostly it is young husbands who speak like that, for older men have discovered that the assumption of male superiority implied in the remark usually produces negative reaction in wives and results in male shamefaced apologies.

Do men and women think differently? Is there male reason and female reason, both right enough in their own way? Or is there male reason and female irrationality? The answer usually given is that men are more rational than women and women more intuitive than men. But this answer does not take us far enough. We have to go on to explain what we mean by *rational,* and that gets us into very deep waters indeed. However, we should search out an answer to the problem.

We can say, surely, that human beings have minds, that their minds have to make sense of the world and their daily experiences, and that the sense they find is communicated in words. Through words we can share one another's experiences—learn through the experiences of other people and teach others what we have learned.

Men and women live on the same planet. They rise each morning to the same new day and sample during the day some of the rich variety that the earth has to offer. This is the world they must understand, and their minds enable them to gain that understanding. The lives of other people can help this process of understanding. When Paul wrote about the mind of Christ being the mind that should be in his disciples—that they should learn from him how to face life—he made no distinction between male and female disciples. Understanding is for men and women alike.

THE LIFE OF THE MIND

Having a life of the mind makes us persons. Growing out of childhood brings problems in different forms to boys and to girls. Growing into persons confronts them with a basically identical problem—developing a mind of their own.

The way in which body and mind grow together is especially obvious at the teen stage. At the time when young people are conscious of becoming sexual beings—with all the perplexities that that brings—they are having to grapple also with an understanding of themselves as potential adults. In front of them they see new responsibilities, not just for managing their own lives but for directing society as well. Knowledge of their physical and mental capabilities causes them to wonder about themselves as persons—individuals different from other individuals, having their own thoughts which are not necessarily shared even by their best friends.

But, above all, they discover that the ideas they have are very different from those of their parents and teachers. They have to be different, of course, because the end of childhood is more than coming to look grown-up. Mostly, it is coming to have *a mind of your own.*

Learning to have a mind of your own is a tremendously hard lesson to learn. No wonder those years are a danger period for suicide, for the near-adult suddenly finds himself faced by problem upon problem only dimly guessed at before. Hearing about other people having to face decisions—people older than yourself and living lives that you take for granted—is one thing. It is another thing altogether to realize that you have to make the decisions facing you because you are *you.*

Life is not made easier for you if your elders, who up to now have made all the important decisions for you, are eager to go on making them. They may even insist upon making them, saying that you have not had enough experience to know what you really want. Earlier in your life you may have wanted your own way without really knowing what you wanted. But now your mind tells you that you have to decide for yourself, even though you haven't had the experience. And, if you keep putting off responsibility, you never will have experience.

No way has been found of knowing when an adolescent is mature enough to know his own mind and is not merely wanting his own way childishly. Often, at this uncertain place, a break in community is necessary in order that young and old may learn to respect each other in a new way and find community again between persons. The break may be less drastic, or even avoided entirely, if the near-adult knows that his elders have always been ready to accept him as a person in his own right.

Conflict can hardly be avoided when parents and teachers *do not know their own minds* and waver between strict authority and lax permissiveness in their attitudes. As this happens in homes, so it can happen for a whole society. The problem of "alienated youth" that has flared up so dramatically on college campuses in recent years seems to have had this beginning. The demand of a new generation to change society, instead of being trained to take its place in the existing society, led to confrontation with violence because the old generation had a divided mind about the values it was trying to teach the young to respect. You can pass on to others only what you believe with all your mind.

WORLDS OF THE MIND: MALE AND FEMALE

All human persons live in the same world; yet no two individuals have exactly the same experiences. So, to a certain extent, each of us has his own world of the mind. This world begins to grow with our earliest memories and takes shape from the sights, sounds, smells, and thoughts that come to us every day. The world of the Eskimo in the loneliness of the Arctic wilderness is far removed from the world of the man hurrying along the busy streets of our North American cities. Similarly, although a business executive and a store clerk may rub shoulders in passing, their worlds are very different also.

Male and female worlds are not too different while boys and girls are learning what life is all about. Parents may try to make the differences show, saying, "Boys don't cry," or "Girls don't play rough games." But, left to themselves, many boys enjoy playing with dolls and many girls enjoy kicking footballs. And all children cry. They imitate their mothers and fathers, of course, and sometimes like to be called "little mothers" or "big men." Pre-adolescent children are eager to imitate *both* parents. For example, a daughter will accompany her father on a fishing trip just as readily as a son will—provided she has not been given the idea that "only men go fishing." In the same way, a son will like helping his mother bake a pie—provided he has not been told that it is "woman's work." It is the *grown-up* role that children want to "try on" rather than a male role or a female role.

Because children learn mainly through imitation, they will adopt distinct male and female roles if the difference is stressed greatly by the adults around them as they grow up. But not otherwise. At the age of four a girl may think that girls wear swim suits with tops just as they wear frilly petticoats when they go to birthday parties. It depends entirely on what she finds expected of her and her friends. Certainly, left to herself, she would jump topless into the swimming pool along with her brothers and never think a thing about it.

In primitive societies boys—and girls to a lesser extent—are prepared for adulthood through extended and often severe initiation ceremonies. Today there is nothing remotely like that outside campus fraternities and sororities, and their purpose is entirely different since they are exclusive and not inclusive. The high school or college graduation is the only ceremony that is used to mark a coming-of-age. The traditional meaning of the twenty-first birthday with its symbol of the key (to go and come as an adult) has almost disappeared. Twenty-one is no longer even the universal age for voting and drinking. But graduation means the same for male and female.

Though he is not prepared by society in any set way to enter the male adult world, the modern male youth does enter it. The world he will live in will be different from the world of his wife. Also, his world will differ subtly from the world he shares outwardly with the women who work where he works. Undefined prejudice against the woman always exists. She will find that equal qualifications will not earn her equal opportunity with a man. Even the woman in the church, whose worth is not measured by salary, will find no equality of treatment. In the very body that affirms men and women are alike before God, they are not treated so. A woman minister has testified to the fact that if she and a man are waiting for an interview, the man will always be admitted first. Professional and business women can supply more evidence of this kind. Part of the problem comes from prejudice, which is not always masculine; part of the problem comes from the woman's not wanting to commit herself wholly to a profession. If she thinks as an amateur, she will be treated as an amateur.

MALE AND FEMALE ROLES

Growing children are told a great deal about what a man should be like and what a woman should be like. But these days much of what they are told will be contradicted by other ideas they hear, or by what they see. Our changing society has produced confusion about male and female roles. Young adults, in particular, have reacted strongly against the ideal of the "he-man" so prominent in American literature, movies, and advertisements. With the slogan "make love, not war," the image of the aggressive male who is quick to settle any argument with his fists has become discredited. And the common complaint of persons over thirty, "you can't tell the boys from the girls," points to the fact that, consciously or unconsciously, many young people want it that way. Unisex fashions reflect a rejection of traditional beliefs about male and female roles.

Among the ideas children hear about male and female roles, one statement likely to make an impression is the one often made in connection with plans for career training: "It doesn't matter so much for a girl, because she probably will get married anyway."

This is the sort of remark that drives supporters of Women's Liberation to fury. But, like it or not, it has a solid basis in reality. Hearing this said—especially by another woman—may cause the girl with strong ambitions in some line of work to realize the extra effort required of her if she is to win her way in a male-dominated world. On the other hand, she may be aware that part of her agrees with the statement, however reactionary this seems. And statistics do support the fact that only a fraction of those women who are qualified to follow a career outside the home continue in it throughout life. Many girls frankly enter college or business school with the intention of meeting some suitable marriage partner. Perhaps this may not be explained entirely as thoughtless acceptance of the way things have been in a society where women were "inferior."

For some women the home and family that marriage brings is an all-sufficient career. Here they find self-fulfillment rather than restriction and frustration. Here they find a role that satisfies and gives them a sense of worth and dignity.

Some women find this in home and marriage; some do not. Is that so very surprising or unnatural? If women are first of all human beings, then all the capacities known in mankind can be seen in them. But not all will be found in each individual. We are able to choose different paths of life because our minds lead us to them and make us wish to follow them. And our minds are as different as our bodies.

Many of our modern problems come from unconscious, or only partly conscious, prejudices about male and female roles. All too often men carry with them the hidden feeling that women are not human beings like themselves and that men alone ought to direct the workings of society. They find it difficult to accept women who come into this "man's world," except when these women stay in obviously subordinate positions: stenographers, telephone operators, cleaners, and machine-minders. Along with this feeling goes the belief that homemaking and bringing up children is women's *real* work, and "subordinate" by position—just as the work that the majority of women do in the male world of industry or business is considered "subordinate" work. Consequently, women who stay at home sense this male attitude and begin to compare their work to that of an unpaid servant.

What we desperately need is a new concept of male and female partnership through all of life. With this concept we shall see that male and female roles *may* be different. A home can be run by a division of labor whereby the man supports his wife so that she can give her full time to her family. But there can also be partnership in work, where men and women, as human beings, play similar roles.

A VARIETY OF MINDS

Minds are very different among human beings, and there is no reason to think that the chief lines of difference run along the divisions of sex. Some human beings—probably the majority of them—are concerned primarily with using their minds to solve the practical problems they meet every day. Others are more curious and inquisitive and like to solve problems for the sake of stretching their minds. Some are fascinated by complicated machines or by numbers and diagrams. Some like to learn how to manage people and organize them to carry out projects. Some meditate on great ideas. Again, some live in their imaginations—write stories, compose music, or paint pictures. Men *and* women do all these things. They find the way of using their minds that comes most readily to them.

The idea that there are some subjects that interest men but bore women (and the other way round) has little to support it. Often we hear said: "Men talk politics and sports, while women talk babies and gossip about the neighbors." This age-old male judgment (which lives on in the comics and in television suburban-life series) indicates a state of affairs that is more artificial than natural. People talk about the subjects that are important in the place where their lives are led. If men are engaged in public life while women spend nearly every hour of their day in the home and hardly go further than the local shopping market, then their conversations will show it.

Very often men are just as limited in their range of interests as the most domesticated woman is. Wives frequently complain that their husbands never talk to them when they come home from work. A silent dinner is followed by switching on the television, and breakfast is another silent meal eaten behind the screen of the morning paper. Clearly, the reason for this is that here the man and the woman live in different mental worlds, and the husband finds conversation outside his own closed world difficult. He avoids the effort.

A newlywed couple was entertaining an older man in the same line of business as the young husband. The wife explained that Harry had a lot of work to bring home each evening while he was getting accustomed to his new job, but she hoped this would not go on too long. The older man looked at Harry and said, with surprise, "But what would you do in the evenings if you didn't have work to see to?"

Perhaps few minds are limited or closed to that extent. Yet it is true that the mental worlds of a working husband and of a wife with a young and demanding family are so different that each is tempted to withdraw into his or her own mental world, forgetting the partnership they should be carrying on. When the children grow up, or when the husband retires, the pair may find to their dismay that they are strangers who have to learn again how to get along together. Exactly the same thing may happen if the wife has a job of her own and has interests outside the house and family. What should matter is that the sense of partnership is never lost. Wherever the two partners of a marriage spend their working day (and only in exceptional circumstances are they likely to spend it together), the important thing is that the two worlds do not pull them apart. They must keep the sense of sharing that gives unity and purpose to all they do.

Once again, sharing does not mean mathematical equality. A marriage must have shared interests if it is to endure. But minds are different, and no law says that two people cannot live happily together unless they have exactly the same tastes and the same interests. If variety is the spice of life, variety of minds is often the spice of marriage. The partnership between a man and a woman is a partnership of persons, and both may find that what they have in common is made richer because they are not afraid of being individuals who sometimes go their own ways and follow their separate interests.

MALE AND FEMALE ATTITUDES

If man has been created in two sorts, male and female, this difference will be noticeable somehow, in every area of life—including the life of the mind.

In the last chapter we discussed Lionel Tiger's views that differences in sex hormones lead to different male and female attitudes toward the world. Dr. Tiger's theory that women are less aggressive than men seems to be borne out by the evidence of history. For instance, the invading of other people's territory has been carried out by male armies, although women were, and are now, frequently found in citizens' armies defending the homeland. Further, automobile insurance companies have found that teen-age male drivers are a bad risk in a way that teen-age female drivers are not.

In mental *ability* there is no difference between male and female, in spite of what long-time male prejudice may say to the contrary. (Quite a number of religions have debated whether woman could have a soul, seemingly believing that her mind was not on an equal level with man.) In mental *attitude* there may be a widespread difference, though not a universal one.

Women's physical role as the carrier and nurturer of life may account for her more realistic attitude toward existence and her frequent suspicions about the male love of abstract thinking—which does not mean that women are not good at abstract thinking if they turn their minds to it. In societies where women are thought to be less intellectual than men, women often have found it more practical to appear to agree than to challenge the reigning prejudice. This simple fact may go far in explaining the myth of the "dumb blond" that still exists among us. If sexual attractiveness is supposed to exclude brains, then the easiest way to be accepted as *womanly* is to act dumb—and play the part intelligently.

So-called "feminine logic" can be explained usually as the woman's practical attitude toward life. Womanly "intuition" often is not intuition at all, but a clear and logical process that jumps some details of an argument to come to the logical conclusion. Intuition may also be the result of close observation of people's behavior rather than of reasons they give to explain their behavior. So a woman may say "trust my intuition" when she cannot easily explain why she decides to do *this* rather than *that*.

The poet Byron wrote:

> Man's love is of man's life a thing apart;
> 'Tis woman's whole existence.
>> (*Don Juan*, I, 194)

Byron may have thought he was proving man to be guided chiefly by reason while woman lived through her emotions. In the female attitude love is very important. Often it has been said, and not unwisely, that in a happy marriage the wife always will be telling her husband how much she admires him, while the husband will find different ways of telling his wife that he loves her. Here again, the practical female attitude becomes apparent. In order to live our lives at all we need to know that we can count on the loving understanding of someone whether or not we are successful.

In the life of the mind, as elsewhere, the male and the female attitudes can complement each other. The human person needs to think both clearly and practically, for we are not disembodied minds; we are living, breathing, feeling beings in whom the intellect needs to be joined to affection and personal understanding.

TEACHING-LEARNING SUGGESTIONS

Topic Question
What is unique about the male mind? And the female mind?

Goal
Decide if and why it is important for you to answer the topic question. You may want to reword the question or to write your own. Then, decide what you want to find out in order to answer your question.

Preview of the Lesson
(This outline of the main ideas in the chapter and the related questions are to aid the leader who chooses the lecture-discussion method of teaching.)

1. Common stereotoypes of men and women attribute a rational mind to the man, an intuitive mind to the woman.
    a. These stereotypes deny that to be human is to have a mind.
    b. To suggest that male and female minds differ because of sex is to deny equal humanity to men and women.
2. The goal of both the man and the woman is to develop a mind of his (her) own.
3. The nature of an individual's mind is based to some extent on the nature of his experiences.
    a. If a child is surrounded by sex-stereotyped experiences, he will adopt these stereotypes through imitation.
    b. Evidence suggests, however, that without these stereotyped images, the male and the female develop alike mentally.
4. Society's role-expectations of the male and the female can affect the individual's "mind of his own."
    a. Women are often limited in educational possibilities because of the supposition that they will not employ their training.
    b. Many men accept women in the business world only in subordinate positions.
    c. Women are suspected of having limited interests; men are attributed broader interests. Differences in interests may be due to differences in experience.

5. Mental abilities are similar for men and women; mental attitudes may differ because of women's role as nurturer of life.
6. The equality of humanity in the male and the female relationship is seen in the sharing as partners between husband and wife.

Related Questions to Discuss
1. What are some stereotypes of the way men think and the way women think? Illustrate these with common expressions.
2. How do you understand the differences between "rational" thinking and "intuitive" thinking? Which is to be preferred? Why?
3. What are some of the barriers you have needed to overcome in trying to develop a mind of your own?
4. How does a man develop a mind of his own? How does a woman? How are these processes alike? How are they different?
5. Once a person has developed a "mind of his own," can he ever lose this characteristic? In what ways might a woman renounce her "mind of her own" when she marries? In what ways might a man?
6. How, specifically, might you help your children develop minds of their own? Would your help be identical for your son and your daughter? Illustrate your answer.
7. How are male and female roles communicated to children in your home? In your public schools? In your church and church school?
8. How do young males and females of today know that they are adults?
9. In what careers is a woman's sex a hindrance to her advancement? In what careers is a woman's sex a legitimate limitation to her participation or advancement?
10. Must a man and a woman share similar mental abilities in order to share equally in the marriage partnership? Why?
11. What do you understand to be the difference between mental ability and mental attitude? Illustrate.

(**The suggestions below are designed to aid leaders and groups desiring a variety of teaching-learning techniques. Choose and adapt those suggestions best suited to the needs of your group.**)
Begin
Commence this session by reflecting on the differences in the education that boys and girls receive. Recall your own school years; what was the attitude toward the girl who wanted to study physics or the boy who studied typewriting? Which subjects were clearly boys' subjects and which clearly girls'? What did these differences say about the understanding of the male and the female mind?

Continue

As a whole group, brainstorm two lists of characteristics, heading one list "Mental Attitudes" and the other list "Mental Abilities." As a result of this listing of characteristics, write a paragraph describing the difference between mental attitudes and mental abilities.

Here is a series of statements that implies an attitude about the difference between men's and women's minds. In groups of four, two men and two women in each group, discuss ways you would respond to these statements as if you were the person being addressed:

"We can't promote you. We never promote women to executive positions because they just get pregnant and have to quit work."

"Let me handle it. What does a man know about comforting a little girl?"

"Sorry, this job calls for a man. We need someone who's willing to commit himself totally to the job and not be worrying about what to get for dinner or about the baby's being sick."

"Let's get a woman to head that committee. It's a job that calls for tact and sensitivity."

Discuss as a whole group responses to these kinds of statements. In your opinion, what has caused these stereotypes of men's and women's mental abilities?

Conclude

Close this session by meditating silently on the final sentence in this chapter, then offer sentence prayers for understanding and insight.

10

the
dimension
of
the spirit

Scripture: 1 Corinthians 2.
The Spirit of God is the final authority for the Christian. The Spirit is our means of knowing God's will for us.

One of the most common complaints heard when a husband and a wife have quarrelled is: "I only said. . . ." "I only said, 'Do you have to wash your hair now?' and she flew at me." "I only said, 'Well, that isn't very funny,' and he wouldn't talk to me for two days."

Actually, those who take pains to justify themselves with the words "I only said" may have said quite a bit more, which they find convenient to forget. Even if their report of the argument is accurate as far as it goes, it hardly ever tells the truth. It does not convey the *spirit* in which the words were spoken. People who know each other well communicate loudly and clearly in ways other than the words they utter. Seemingly harmless words can be like dynamite to ears that are tuned to what lies behind the words.

Jesus was recognizing this when he said that men would be accountable on the day of judgment for every thoughtless word they spoke, because the words men speak come from the overflowing of the heart (Matthew 12:34b-37). Our spirit is our real self and shows the nature of our heart. When James and John wished to call down fire from heaven upon the people who would not receive their Master, Jesus rebuked them, telling them that they did not know what spirit they belonged to (Luke 9:51-55, KJV). We can receive the Holy Spirit, or we can shut our hearts against Him.

THE HUMAN SPIRIT

The human spirit is not always to be thought of as separate from the human mind, because the mind is more than a thinking machine. Our minds are bound up with our self-awareness, and so with everything that we are. When Paul told Christians that they should have the mind that was in Christ Jesus (Philippians 2:5), he could as well have said "spirit." To have the mind of Christ is to be united with his Spirit.

Mankind was created in the image of God. Thus the mind or consciousness (self-awareness) is more than mental ability; it has a spiritual dimension. We are, therefore, spiritual beings. We show our spiritual capacities not only when we worship God, who is Spirit, but also when we forget him and deny his Spirit entry into our lives. Man is never simply a wise or an ignorant being. He is always either a God-fearing or a God-defying one. He can rise to be a saint, or he can sink to be a devil—there is no middle ground. That is why in the Christian life there never can be complacency about human sin. That part of us that is not possessed by the Holy Spirit is ruled by "the spirit of this world." Wherever in our lives we quench the Spirit, there we fight against the purposes of God. Sins of the spirit are never small sins. That is why spiritual pride is considered the most deadly of all sins. The higher we seek to rise in the spiritual dimension, the lower we may fall.

One fact divides the mental life from the spiritual life. Our minds, like our bodies, vary. Some bodies are much stronger than others. Our bodies and our minds alike decay and lose their vigor. But the spirit does not depend upon either body or mind for its power. Here all persons, so differently endowed in everything else, stand before their Maker on the same level. The gift of the Spirit, when received, can make the lowliest, most deprived life glorious. When the Spirit is refused, the most gifted of mankind can lose their sense of worth as human beings.

The Spirit makes no distinctions among persons. Paul makes this point with wonderful simplicity and power:

> There is neither Jew nor Greek, there is neither slave nor free, there is neither male nor female; for you are all one in Christ Jesus. (Galatians 3:28)

God made the world full of variety—one might even say gloriously unequal variety. Even mankind was made in two sorts: male and female. Yet, in the Spirit there are no divisions, not even the division between male and female. In their spirits men and women are simply individuals standing in the presence of God. Here mankind finds its place of true and perfect unity.

RECOGNIZING THE DIMENSION OF THE SPIRIT

In most situations in life we overlook the spirit dimension in persons. We pay little attention to the spirit in which something is done, and much attention to whether it was done the way we wished. We value people for what we can get out of them rather than for what they are in themselves (in their spirit). We use people rather than respect them as spiritual beings like ourselves, made in the image of God.

We overlook the spiritual dignity of others in our daily contacts with them. Much of modern living takes place on the impersonal level; there we treat men and women simply as means to an end. The man at the gas station who fills our automobile tank, the woman at the reception desk who arranges for us to have an interview with her boss, the clerk at the supermarket, the stewardess on the airplane: these are all people from whom we demand service, and we complain if we fail to get as much as we expect. The service we expect is of the kind that might be provided for us by a machine. And, on occasion, when we do remember that we are dealing with human beings rather than with machines, it is probably only because we know we will get better results. Dealing with people on an impersonal level affects our attitudes and makes them dependent on our using people to get what we want. Unfortunately, this happens frequently. Advice about "how to win friends and influence people" nearly always takes this spirit-destroying form. If we introduce a "human" note, such as learning a person's first name or taking notice of persons simply to make them more willing to do what we want them to do, then we are using them as if they were machines. We are also showing our contempt for them by pretending to recognize the human spirit in them. An even more cynical and humanly destructive side of the same attitude emerges when people cultivate private friendships with persons who will be useful to them. Making friends in order to use them is a mockery of the very meaning of friendship.

The greatest sin against the human spirit comes when we carry the attitude of using people into family relationships. In the past, many societies judged a man's importance by the number of wives he could afford to maintain. Polygamy quite openly regarded the woman as the possession of her husband. While this expression of male supremacy is no longer socially acceptable, the attitude underlying it is by no means dead. A wife is still often considered a social and professional asset to her husband; and some women, though no longer bought and sold, continue to allow themselves to be acquired and displayed as though they were a valuable piece of property. A mercenary relationship in marriage is based on use rather than respect; it denies the spirit and stifles human relationships.

Most of us are not tempted to buy or sell men and women for money or position. But the basic temptation to use those around us rather than to respect their spiritual personhood is constant enough. Some husbands and wives use their mates quite ruthlessly for their own purposes, never allowing them to become persons in their own right. The husband who sacrifices his wife's happiness to his career and the wife who demands that her husband devote himself to satisfying her own wants are equally common and equally ruthless. Using another person may take the form of crude bullying—the undisguised assertion of a strong will over a weak one—or it may appear as a show of weakness and dependency—appealing to the "unselfish" nature of the partner who is being enslaved. In either event the result is that the one uses the other as a means to his or her self-assertion. One spirit is killed, while the other spirit grows in a distorted and devilish form.

THE COMMUNITY OF THE SPIRIT

Every failure to recognize and trust the spirit in another is a perversion of the spirit in the one who wishes to use the other person.

We can see this from the examples mentioned above. As persons we are dependent upon the community of persons. We can become ourselves only through the process of giving and receiving within the community of mankind: in families, in neighborhoods, and in nations. And we need guidance, support, encouragement, and correction if we are to understand the spirit that is in us and distinguish between the Spirit of God and the spirit of self-seeking.

Only a fine line separates genuine partnership from exploitation and loving care from smothering domination. In a marriage, the two partners are not likely to be equally strong-minded or strong-willed. Out of this inequality a loving partnership can be made when each partner sees and respects in the other an individual spirit, different in its strengths and weaknesses, and wishes that spirit to be expressed at its best. The differences can be the foundation upon which mutual support is built, provided the partners are bound by a common spirit of love. Where this common spirit is lacking, the stronger partner will try to dominate the weaker one, and the weaker partner will try to escape domination by falsehood and evasion. Either way, the partnership will be destroyed.

Always it is the presence of the spirit of trust within a community that prevents it from disintegrating, that keeps it whole in periods of crisis. If the spirit of trust is lacking, a community is like a house built on sand, ready to collapse at the slightest disturbance. At the beginning of this chapter we mentioned the phrase "I only said . . . ," which marks so many breakdowns in family communication. The people who voice the "I-only-said" complaint are really saying that they live in a situation where the spirit of trust does not exist; anything or nothing may occasion a complete break in their personal relationships.

Love between persons has a physical basis; it grows out of sexual attraction and out of the intimacies of the family situation of living, eating, and sleeping together. Love has a mental side also; it is strengthened by learning from one another and by sharing common interests and a common outlook upon the world because of being together in a closely knit community. But, primarily, love is a spiritual thing; it cannot last if the spirit of one individual does not go out to the spirit of another, acknowledging the infinite worth of that spirit—unique and irreplaceable, not to be compelled or commanded but to be trusted and true to itself. Love is not just a feeling, even a feeling of good will; it is living in the spirit of trust in the other who is different, and being different, able as an individual to return that trust.

Hear what Paul says about the gifts of the Spirit that individuals bring to the life of the church:

> There are varieties of gifts, but the same Spirit. There are varieties of service, but the same Lord. There are many forms of work, but all of them, in all men, are the work of the same God. In each of us the Spirit is manifested in one particular way, for some useful purpose . . .

But all these gifts are the work of one and the same Spirit,
distributing them separately to each individual at will.
(I Corinthians 12:4-9, 11, NEB)

What Paul writes about work within the Christian church
applies as well to all relationships within the human community. Love, "the more excellent way" for human life,
blossoms only where the differences in individuals are
valued as gifts of the Spirit of God, reflected in the human
spirit and uniting mankind in a common spirit.

UNITY IN THE SPIRIT

Because we are spiritual beings, as well as beings with
bodies and minds, that which most forcefully unites or
divides us belongs to the spirit. We are speaking not only
of our religious faith, but of all convictions that we hold
about the nature of the universe and our place in it.

Marriage between persons of different faiths has always
been—and still is—a cause for heart searching. Admittedly,
the question is not as thorny as it used to be. In previous
times, religious faith was not merely a matter of belonging
to a certain religious denomination or holding to a particular creed. Rather, it was a way of life within the community,
and to marry someone of another faith was to join oneself
with a stranger, an outsider to one's way of life. This situation still exists, to some extent, when a practicing Jew
marries a gentile; but in our culture religious faith has
become largely an individual concern. Religious "mixed
marriages" may experience less strain than marriages involving two persons of widely different economic back-
grounds or of divergent political views.

Religion today is not thought to be the divisive force it
once was; neither is it thought to be an essential uniting
force. Yet, the uniting of two spirits in a partnership can
hardly take place if they view the meaning of their lives
in conflicting ways. In the nineteen-thirties, when religion
counted for less than it does at the present time—in Europe
at least—the European psychologist Carl Jung said that he
had never seen a patient over forty years of age whose real
problem was not, at bottom, religious. Almost certainly,
that is true now.

More than a thousand years ago Augustine, the great
North African bishop, wrote: "Thou hast made us for

Thyself, and our hearts are restless until they find their rest in Thee" (*Confessions*, I, i). Men and women were created by God to live in fellowship with their Maker and with their brothers and sisters in the human community. When part of the divine intention for mankind is fulfilled, then that part of community is realized upon earth. Thus marriage and the family circle can be satisfying and harmonious to the extent to which a true community of human spirits comes into existence. In truth, religious belief is not the *sole* foundation for human partnership. Many couples manage to get along very well together on the basis of human values alone, without recognizing any transcendent purpose for their lives. Further, having religious belief does not exempt men and women from the strains and breakdowns that beset all human relationships.

However, if Augustine was right, then faith is not optional for human beings in their search for true community. Unless we receive the gift of the Spirit of God, our own spirits will turn in upon themselves and become perverted.

Not by accident does the New Testament speak of the *grace* of our Lord Jesus Christ, the *love* of God, and the *communion* or *fellowship* of the *Holy Spirit* (2 Corinthians 13:14). God's Holy Spirit unites us with God and with our neighbors.

For Christian believers, unity in the Spirit keeps intact the bond of peace (Ephesians 4:3). We can walk together and keep together when we have the gift that "is from above, coming down from the Father" (James 1:17), which is the gift of his Spirit.

THE HARVEST OF THE SPIRIT

The gift of God's spirit bears fruit in us. Paul describes it this way: "But the harvest of the Spirit is love, joy, peace, patience, kindness, goodness, fidelity, gentleness, and self-control" (Galatians 5:22-23, NEB). And he adds, "There is no law dealing with such things as these."

Laws never deal with the innermost problems arising out of our misuse of our created nature. At best, legislation by governments or unwritten rules laid down by public opinion can prevent the worst abuses of inhumanity and cruelty. But, all too often, laws simply maintain the state of affairs brought about by the hardness of men's hearts.

God's Holy Spirit alone, coming "from above" to remake our fallen nature, can restore the right relationship between men and women, parents and children, families and neighboring families, nation and nation.

Because our human spirits are constantly in opposition to the Divine Spirit, we experience *spirituality* only in scattered moments. Were the harvest of the Spirit allowed to come to ripeness in us, then what we call religion would be part of our everyday life and not divided from anything that we do. As it is, our lives and our religious faith often exist in separate compartments, unable to flow into each other and color our whole existence with spiritual grace. This is why we need to be reminded constantly of the Spirit of God that is alien to the spirit of the world and to be reminded of our need to repent and to discover the new life that God's spirit offers.

Those who say that they can be good without being religious may be right, as far as their expectations go. Churchgoing that is merely routine or religious gesture will not open us to the Spirit. But the practice of religious faith is something we all need if we are to avoid becoming deaf and blind to the promptings of the Spirit. Religious faith is a continual call to open our ears and eyes to a reality otherwise easy to ignore.

Wherever the fruit of the Spirit is found, God has been at work bringing the human spirit to Himself through his reconciling grace. But a life constantly showing these fruits is rare indeed. Even in the Christian church, created to be the fellowship of the Spirit, such lives are the exception rather than the rule. But that is no reason for thinking the church to be unnecessary. Rather, we should take seriously the message that the church gives to every generation, a message that we cannot hear except from the church. This is the message of the grace of our Lord Jesus Christ, the love of God, and the fellowship of the Spirit.

In the church, imperfect and inward-turned though it is, the prayer is raised, "Come, Holy Spirit."

TEACHING-LEARNING SUGGESTIONS

Topic Question
What is the spirit of a man or the spirit of a woman, and what part does it play in the life of either?

Goal
Decide if and why it is important for you to answer the topic question. You may want to reword the question or to write your own. Then, decide what you want to find out in order to answer your question.

Preview of the Lesson
(This outline of the main ideas in the chapter and the related questions are to aid the leader who chooses the lecture-discussion method of teaching.)

1. The spiritual dimension of persons affects personal life, whether the individual recognizes it or not.
2. While persons may vary in physical and mental characteristics, everyone—male and female—is equal in spirit before God.
3. We are called to recognize the spirit of all other persons as the evidence of God within them.
   a. When we seek to use persons for our own gains, we are denying them the uniqueness of their spirit.
      1. We use and manipulate persons whenever we see them as less than our totally human partners under God.
      2. We use persons within our families when we are forcing our expectations on our children or forcing our spouses to assume our ideal of their roles.
   b. Manipulating others destroys the spirit both of the person being used and of the person who is using another.
4. Within the marriage, husband and wife must share the same spirit; otherwise, the stronger will dominate the weaker.
5. Only the spirit within a community—the attitude of mutual trust—holds a community together.
6. Love is the reaching *out* of the spirit of one person *to* the spirit of another.
7. As spirit can unite us as nothing else can, so can spirit divide us.

Related Questions to Discuss
1. When have you seen the spirit of a person contradict his words?
2. How can we open our spirits to the influence of the Holy Spirit?
3. What is the difference between being possessed by the

Holy Spirit and being ruled by "the spirit of this world?" How can you know which spirit controls your life?

4. How do persons use other persons? Give examples.

5. Is a husband more likely to use his wife? Or the wife her husband? Give reasons for answering as you do.

6. What experiences or situations might destroy or kill a woman's spirit? A man's spirit? If your answers are different for these two questions, how do you explain that difference?

7. How does using another person destroy the spirit of that person? Of the person who uses the other?

8. How might a community develop a spirit of trust among its members? How is the spirit of trust between husbands and wives like a spirit of trust within a community?

9. In what ways has religion, a matter of the spirit, been used to divide persons? How might religion be used to unite persons?

10. Must persons be of the same religion to be of the same spirit? Why or why not?

11. What must a man do to be open to the Holy Spirit? What must a woman do? Is the religion of a man different from the religion of a woman? Illustrate your answer.

(The suggestions below are designed to aid leaders and groups desiring a variety of teaching-learning techniques. Choose and adapt those suggestions best suited to the needs of your group.)
Begin

Divide into two groups, one consisting of men, the other of women. Let each group discuss these questions: Are men more religious than women? Are women more religious than men? Reflect on participation in your local church as you consider this question. If you consider one sex to be more religious than the other, do you also consider that sex to be more spiritual than the other? Carefully explain the reasons for your answer. Now let the men and women share and compare their discussion. Do both groups generally agree? Why or why not?

Continue

Act out some situations in which either husband or wife uses his or her spouse, denying the spirit of that person. You may want to portray the self-centered husband who doubts that his wife can do anything but serve him, or the wife who controls her husband by feigning sickness constantly. Indicate and role play other situations. Is the person who is being used always aware that he or she is being used? Might a person ever choose to be used? Why? What changes would have to be made in the relationships you portrayed to recast them as shared relationships between husbands and wives who respected the spirit of one another?

Consider what the writers call the "fine line separating genuine partnership from exploitation" (page 139). Can you as a whole group list a number of characteristics on which all agree that would help a couple determine just where that "fine line" is for them?

Discuss as a whole group: How is the growing boy's spirit different from the growing girl's spirit? How is the nurture of a girl's spirit different from the nurture of a boy's spirit? Illustrate your answer with examples.

Conclude

Read silently the paragraph about the nature of love (p. 140). Then let several members of the group summarize their understanding and definition of love, using insights from this paragraph.

11
life
in
the
church

LEO M. JOHNSON

Scripture: Matthew 16:15-20; Ephesians 5:25-32
The Church is Christ's creation and the object
of his love, just as human love finds its object
in the marriage relation between man and
woman.

In Christ's church mankind is called into unity of fellow-ship and newness of life. New life in Christ comes through leaving behind the old, fallen nature that "is sinking towards death" (Ephesians 4:22, NEB).

Yet we do not now live fully in Christ and under the guidance of the Holy Spirit. Our hardness of heart has entered the community of grace, turning it too often into a likeness of the fallen world. Instead of oneness in Christ, we have competing denominations. Instead of the truth held in love, we have conflicting opinions and rival creeds. Instead of partnership in the faith, we have private ambitions working through cliques and church politics. Instead of the reconciliation of all men confessing the Lordship of Jesus, we have divisions along national and regional boundaries or based on class and race.

All forms of Christianity have been imperfect embodiments of the community of which Christ is the head. Jesus Christ called the church that he loved to be "holy and without blemish" (Ephesians 5:27). The churches we know are very unlike that. From the first, Christ's church has been made up of people who, in Paul's words, are "babes in Christ," taking the first faltering steps along the new path of life to which they have been called. But they are old in the ways of the world, and they slip back readily into the fashions of the world's thinking and acting.

Church people can easily be condemned for their poor performance, when measured against the high claims that the New Testament makes for the church of Christ. We find it easy to say that the churches have failed and that they have nothing to offer. We speak quickly of complacency, hypocrisy, and irrelevancy. The charges are mostly accurate enough, for they are charges against the presence of fallen human nature in the fellowship of those who have been summoned to a higher way.

Yet the one failing that is fatal for the church is to lose faith in the message entrusted to it. The church can survive its other faults—and they are many—provided it remembers that it is answerable to God alone and does not try to justify itself by a kind of "relevance" or success that the world approves and applauds. The church is not a place where model Christians are exhibited to convince the world that Christianity works. The church is the place where grace is working with imperfect material, the place where the need for repentance is remembered and the power of God is available in weakness.

If we want to see evidence of human sin and folly, we certainly can find that in the life of the churches. But if we have eyes to look for the working of the Holy Spirit among mankind, we shall find that too. The churches have no monopoly on either moral uprightness or moral corruption. However, in the churches, and there alone, people are pointed to the life of the spirit as the goal of existence, and to the Spirit of Christ as the present reality and the hope of mankind. The prayer of the Christian church is not "We have arrived" but "Thy Kingdom come."

MEN AND WOMEN IN THE CHURCH

In Christ, says Paul, there is neither male nor female. Yet, as the world has come into the churches and left its mark there, so the divisions developed in the world between male and female appear there also.

Every congregation is both the local embodiment of the universal church of Jesus Christ and a cultural institution reflecting the prejudices and limitations of contemporary society. Paul, for example, understood that the spiritual unity of mankind in Christ abolishes all difference between human beings, including the differences of sex. Yet being a man of his time, he discouraged women from taking an active part in the services of the local congregations. And since his time the cultural forces leading to the subjection of women to the male ego have been quite evident in all churches—especially the highly organized, well-known ones. Ironical as it is, in a day when other professions have opened the door to women, the professional ministries of the large denominations are still mostly a male preserve.

However, at the present it appears that the feminist movement may triumph in the churches also. For example, in the Roman Catholic Church, that most conservative of all churchly institutions, the admission of women to the priesthood is being discussed seriously. A long interval may lapse, of course, between discussion of the principles involved and any actual move to put those principles into action. Yet the fact remains that ideas that would have been unthinkable a few years ago are now being actively considered.

Changes of this kind are nearly always the result of pressure from the "world" upon the churches, rather than the other way around. This is not surprising since the organization of churches reflects the thinking of people in a culture at a particular time in history. In a sense, organization is the "flesh" of the churches; and, as Jesus said, "the spirit indeed is willing, but the flesh is weak" (Matthew 26:41). This has been true of the process by which Christians have worked out their spiritual convictions in their institutions. Two thousand years of Christian history show this pattern of "cultural lag." As Paul's letter to Philemon makes clear, the early Christians learned to accept a Christian slave as a brother, yet they never challenged the institution of slavery, which was an accepted part of their cultural life. So it was with the status of women.

Women played a prominent part in New Testament history, but the social structure of the time made unthinkable any notion that women could be *leaders* in the new movement. While women were associated with the Apostles, and thus at the heart of the movement, the Twelve chosen by Jesus were men. And the early church grew wholly directed by males.

However, the spiritual equality of men and women was taken for granted. Along with males, female saints and martyrs were honored by Christians in the years of persecution under the Roman government. This attitude has continued throughout the history of the church. In the roll of great names of Christians, women's names mingle with the names of men down through the centuries.

WOMEN IN CHURCH HISTORY

A common complaint heard today is that women outnumber men in the churches. The lack of men in congregations is often used as an argument to show the present "irrelevance" of the church and its failure to be "meaning-ful" to contemporary man.

This judgment is an example of the male ego at work, for it springs from the questionable view that an institution is important only if it attracts male support. What is inter-esting about this view is that the people who voice the opinion that the church has failed because it is supported by "old women" (presumably, instead of by young male executives) are also those who express strong disapproval of the times when religion was a leading concern of the men of power and prestige, when popes and bishops made and destroyed kings and emperors. "We are not living in the Middle Ages," they say. Yet, from the way in which they speak of the "failure" of the churches, one would imagine they would like to be.

Confusing spiritual strength with worldly power is evidently a common error, especially among male minds.

Throughout the history of the Christian church (and perhaps all religions) women have been the mainstay of the practice of Christian life and Christian worship, even though they have been denied positions of leadership except under male direction. This fact may be closely con-nected to women's more practical and realistic understand-ing of existence. As we saw earlier, the male mind runs more readily to abstract reasoning and the construction of theories than does the female mind. Just as the world's greatest philosophers have been men—and even today few women are attracted to this field—so theology is almost exclusively an interest of males. But in the day-to-day living of the life of faith, and in the handing down of faith to the next generation, women have always surpassed men.

When Paul wrote of Timothy's standing in the faith, he called him his "son." Yet he attributed Timothy's spiritual strength not to himself but to Timothy's mother and grand-mother. A long succession of notable Christian mothers stand as the inspiration of countless great men in Christian history—a much more illustrious roll than that of Christian fathers! We know Augustine's mother, Monica, because of his tribute to her in his *Confessions*.

Also noteworthy is the fact that these Christian women were *seldom* only shadowy presences standing in the background as good influences for their famous sons. They were nearly always individual *personalities* in their own right. Monica stands out in Augustine's *Confessions* as a person we could recognize and not just as the woman "behind" Augustine. John Wesley's mother, Susanna, was another strong personality, though of a very different kind. And St. Teresa of Avila is far more real to us as a person than are the great majority of the medieval male saints. Other famous Christian women give evidence of the same power of being themselves above everything.

What these examples from history show is that, within cultures where women seldom moved outside the circle of home and family, social and institutional limitations did not prevent *all* women from reaching the highest level of personal development. Perhaps the lesson to be learned is that individuals become real persons through the freeing of their spirits, whether or not they are acknowledged by the society in which they live.

THE FEMALE CONTRIBUTION TO SPIRITUALITY

To the ardent feminist, of course, history teaches quite another lesson. The fact that men gain all the headlines of history while women usually find a place as a footnote to masculine fame is, to the feminist, clear evidence of a male conspiracy to keep women in subjection and to deprive them of their status as persons. In the opinion of the feminist, women who have accepted masculine enslavement and who have been content to sacrifice themselves so that their husbands and sons might gain fame and power have betrayed their own sex and have helped maintain male domination.

Indeed it is true that women have been treated unjustly throughout history, and the gifts of mind and imagination possessed by countless women were never allowed expression in society at large. What is not so certain is that it was social conditioning, pure and simple, that made women willing to subordinate themselves to men. The idea that women, either in the past or in the present, accept a less prominent role in society because they have been brainwashed by males is far from proven.

If women are more concerned with personal existence than with abstract theorizing, they may have good reason to doubt that all the questions of the relationship between the sexes hinge on the idea of equality. They may see the drive toward social achievement and fame as something more characteristic of the masculine personality than of the feminine personality, and therefore as pointing to a natural division of function in human society. A woman's willingness to subordinate herself to her menfolk may then be a sign of strength rather than one of weakness and servility. She has grasped the meaning of the teaching of Jesus that whoever would be great in the kingdom of heaven must be ready to be humbled, to serve instead of being served.

Such an attitude is not necessarily a betrayal of her sex because the woman who follows this course does not sacrifice herself to man in the abstract. She does not assume that, just because she is a woman, she is less gifted than a man. She does what she does, if she acts as a real person, out of love and concern and not because "a woman's place is in the home."

The feminist's insistence that every woman is a person in her own right and not simply an adjunct to some male is right as far as it goes. But it does not go far enough. For it would seem to wipe out all distinctions between maleness and femaleness, reducing the differences to "accidental" physical ones. Such a view fails to take seriously the fact that mankind has been created in two sorts. And it fails to understand that the human person is never complete in isolation, but finds fullness in partnership.

If men are to accept the true humanity of women, then they cannot assume any natural male superiority. Futher, they must be prepared to accept women as equal partners in work, where women choose a public career. But they also must acknowledge the feminine as the complement to the masculine, accepting—not as a right but as a privilege—the service of women when this is a woman's choice.

Women's inclination toward spirituality leads them to see existence in terms of service to God. This is why they, more than men, understand the place of faith in life and the place of the church in the community. For many women, a life of service to the family is taken as a matter of course with little thought given to the reasons. They find real and personal satisfaction in their sacrificial caring for the well-being of the members of their families. But for many others, love of family is rooted in the love of God.

Male cynics claim that women turn to good works in the churches to make up for the poverty of their lives, or because they are naturally superstitious. Cynics about human nature are not mistaken every time; but they seldom see more than a small part of the truth, and they usually get that out of focus. The spiritual dedication of women is a constant fact of history and cannot be explained away. This dedication is found in the happily married as well as in the single. A much more likely explanation of a woman's concern for faith lies in woman's ability to face facts and to realize that the most important of all facts must be the fact of God and his claim upon our service.

MALE AND FEMALE AT ONE IN CHRIST

The unity we find in Christ is "in the Spirit." Because we share the same Spirit—God's Spirit given through Christ —we become as one in his church. Yet, as long as we live in our bodies we are not just spirit. Our humanness, and so our male and female natures, enters into all we are and all we do. This is why the family relationship, which arises out of the various physical needs of human beings, is used so often in the Bible as a guide to our spiritual situation. Children, growing up to become adult persons in their own right, need the love and care of parents. So Jesus taught his disciples to speak of God as their Father who knows every need of his children. In a sense God is both father and mother to his children. "As one whom his mother comforts, so I will comfort you" (Isaiah 66:13). But, since pagan worship of mother goddesses as embodiments of the sexual power in nature was common in both Old Testament and New Testament times, the title of Mother is never applied to God in the Bible. God is beyond both maleness and femaleness. He is the creator of sexuality but is not sexual in his own personhood.

Similarly, Paul describes the relation between Christ and his church as the relationship between a husband and a wife. Again, the comparison goes beyond sexuality. Christ is husband in the sense that he chooses the church as his partner and cares for it with the same intimate love that exists between husband and wife in a true marriage partnership. In the Christian church we learn about God, Jesus Christ, and the Holy Spirit; it is there that we are brought into the family of God. So the comparison of Christ and his church to husband and wife naturally leads to our speaking of the church as a mother. While this way of speaking has been more common among Roman Catholics than among Protestants, it was the great Protestant reformer John Calvin who said, "No one can have God as his Father who does not have the Church as his Mother." And we sing at our worship:

> The Church's one foundation
> Is Jesus Christ *her* Lord.

Perhaps we would understand better our need for the church if we thought of it more often as *Mother* church.

The life of faith is that life in which people find themselves fully as persons. Thus, "in the Spirit," men and women have exactly the same needs. There is no male or female way of finding God, no male or female way of receiving the Holy Spirit. At the same time, the male and female aspects of personality are so much a part of our human experience that they do enter into our experience of spiritual concerns.

We have examined the way in which women seem more receptive than men to the dimension of the spirit, because of their greater experience of personal relationships at the individual level. In the mother-child relationship there is a more personal concern for the individual who is to become responsible in the next generation than there usually is in the father-child relationship. What we have said about the importance of the Christian mother is recognized also in the parent faith of Christianity. In the case of children of mixed marriages between Jews and gentiles, an individual is said to belong to the Jewish faith when his or her mother (not father) is Jewish and this in spite of the very strong emphasis in Judaism upon the father-son relationship.

In the cultivation of the spiritual life in the church, sexuality cannot be ignored, though it can be transcended. The basis of the fellowship within the church that looks forward to the coming of God's kingdom as the universal community is the mutual dependence and trust existing between members of a family. There, differences exist:

differences of age, mental powers, natural talents, and sex. But, in the end, none of these matter since it is the community of love between persons that makes the family a unity. Through sharing, through willingness to sacrifice, and through forgiving understanding, family oneness is preserved—and passed on to the next generation to build other family communities. In the same way, though with a more universal purpose, the family of the church should build the sharing experience that brings persons to know themselves as sons and daughters of the family of God.

TEACHING-LEARNING SUGGESTIONS

Topic Question
What are distinctive contributions of men and of women in the church?

Goal
Decide if and why it is important for you to answer the topic question. You may want to reword the question or to write your own. Then, decide what you want to find out in order to answer your question.

Preview of the Lesson
(This outline of the main ideas in the chapter and the related questions are to aid the leader who chooses the lecture-discussion method of teaching.)

1. The Christian gospel calls persons into the unity of fellowship and newness of life through the church.
   a. But persons, accustomed to the spirit of the world, fall back constantly from the way of the gospel.
   b. Persons are tempted to lose faith in the message of the church.
2. In Christ, there is neither male nor female.
   a. Because the world was divided sexually, however, the church became divided sexually with the men dominant.
   b. The present culture is pressuring the church to grant full partnership to women.
3. Women have been outstanding in church history.
   a. Women are prominent in both the Old and New Testaments.
   b. Strong women played significant roles in the lives of Christians such as Augustine and Wesley.
4. Women are the mainstay of the practice of the Christian life.
   a. Women are more practical-minded than men.

    b. Women nurture new life and communicate the faith to children.

    c. Women see existence in terms of service to God because they possess a greater spirituality than men.

5. A woman may choose to subordinate herself to her home and family out of a deep understanding of Christian servanthood.

6. God is neither male nor female; he is beyond both, the creator of sexuality, not a sexual being himself.

7. Sexuality cannot be ignored, but it can be transcended in the community of shared partnership between men and women.

Related Questions to Discuss

1. What do you understand to be the message of the church for the unity of mankind?

2. What might cause men to lose their faith in the church's message? What might cause women to lose this faith?

3. Should women have leadership roles in the church similar to the roles men assume? Give reasons for your answer.

4. What volunteer tasks in your church are usually assumed by men? Which by women? Why?

5. Why have women been the mainstay of the practice of Christian life? What is there about the nature of women that makes them more spiritually minded than men?

6. How can a woman reach her highest level of personal development despite the prejudices of society? How can a man overcome cultural stereotypes and find his highest level of development?

7. Why might a woman choose to subordinate herself to her husband and family? Would such a woman be rejecting her own personal development in doing so? Give reasons for your answers.

8. What does it mean to say that "God is beyond both maleness and femaleness . . . not sexual in his own personhood?" What does this statement do to your understanding of God?

9. Should God always be addressed as masculine? Why? What effect might this practice have on a woman's understanding of herself?

10. What specific steps might your church take in order to recognize more completely the life of the spirit and the fellowship of shared humanity?

(The suggestions below are designed to aid leaders and groups desiring a variety of teaching-learning techniques. Choose and adapt those suggestions best suited to the needs of your group.)

Begin

    Commence this session by allowing the men to describe their thoughts and feelings as they read this chapter. What specific statements made by the writers generated doubts and questions for the men? After the men have discussed briefly their reactions to this chapter, the women may wish to ask questions for clarification or to make comments regarding the chapter.

Continue

Carefully discuss the role of women in your local church. To what extent are women part of the decision-making processes in your congregation? What leadership positions seem closed to women in your church, and why? What problems might a female pastor face in your congregation that a male pastor might not face?

Hear a report from your pastor or from a previously assigned group member on women in Christian history. Such a report should include brief discussions of St. Helena, Monica, Susannah Wesley, and others. How has hearing such a report helped you understand the spiritual-mindedness of women?

Working as a whole group, prepare parallel lists describing the contributions of men and women to the kingdom of God through the church. Head one list "The Man's Role in the Service of God" and the other "The Woman's Role in the Service of God." From working on these lists, can you as a group write a paragraph summarizing how men and women work in partnership and complement each other in the service of God?

Conclude

Return to the topic question posted throughout this study: "What does it mean to be a man or a woman?" Let several persons indicate how they would answer this question and how their answer has changed as a result of this study.

Close with sentence prayers for greater sensitivity to the Spirit of God.